Cambridge Elements ⁼

Elements in the Philosophy of Physics
edited by
James Owen Weatherall
University of California, Irvine

LAWS OF PHYSICS

Eddy Keming Chen
University of California, San Diego

CAMBRIDGE
UNIVERSITY PRESS

CAMBRIDGE
UNIVERSITY PRESS

Shaftesbury Road, Cambridge CB2 8EA, United Kingdom

One Liberty Plaza, 20th Floor, New York, NY 10006, USA

477 Williamstown Road, Port Melbourne, VIC 3207, Australia

314–321, 3rd Floor, Plot 3, Splendor Forum, Jasola District Centre,
New Delhi – 110025, India

103 Penang Road, #05–06/07, Visioncrest Commercial, Singapore 238467

Cambridge University Press is part of Cambridge University Press & Assessment,
a department of the University of Cambridge.

We share the University's mission to contribute to society through the pursuit of
education, learning and research at the highest international levels of excellence.

www.cambridge.org
Information on this title: www.cambridge.org/9781009479356

DOI: 10.1017/9781009026390

First published 2024

A catalogue record for this publication is available from the British Library.

ISBN 978-1-009-47935-6 Hardback
ISBN 978-1-009-01272-0 Paperback
ISSN 2632-413X (online)
ISSN 2632-4121 (print)

Cambridge University Press & Assessment has no responsibility for the persistence
or accuracy of URLs for external or third-party internet websites referred to in this
publication and does not guarantee that any content on such websites is, or will
remain, accurate or appropriate.

Laws of Physics

Elements in the Philosophy of Physics

DOI: 10.1017/9781009026390
First published online: June 2024

Eddy Keming Chen
University of California, San Diego

Author for correspondence: Eddy Keming Chen, eddykemingchen@ucsd.edu

Abstract: Despite its apparent complexity, our world seems to be governed by simple laws of physics. This Element provides a philosophical introduction to such laws. It explains how they are connected to some of the central issues in philosophy, such as ontology, possibility, explanation, induction, counterfactuals, time, determinism, and fundamentality. The Element suggests that laws are fundamental facts that govern the world by constraining its physical possibilities. I examine three hallmarks of laws – simplicity, exactness, and objectivity – and discuss whether and how they may be associated with laws of physics.

This element also has a video abstract: www.cambridge.org/Chen

Keywords: time, constraint, simplicity, explanation, modality

ISBNs: 9781009479356 (HB), 9781009012720 (PB), 9781009026390 (OC)
ISSNs: 2632-413X (online), 2632-4121 (print)

Contents

1 Introduction

Much work in physics has been devoted to the discovery of its true fundamental laws: the basic principles that govern the world.[1] The collection of all such laws may be called the axioms of the final theory of physics or the Theory of Everything (TOE). The fundamental laws cannot be explained in terms of deeper principles (Weinberg 1992, p.18). We use them to explain observed phenomena, including the formation of galaxies, the collisions of black holes, the stability of matter, the tidal periods of ocean waves, and the melting of ice cubes.

Laws are intimately connected to many long-standing philosophical issues, such as modality, explanation, causation, counterfactuals, time, induction, and determinism. For example, physical possibility and necessity can be defined in terms of laws; laws contribute to scientific explanations of natural phenomena; laws support counterfactuals, predictions, and retrodictions; laws are linked to the direction of time; determinism and indeterminism are properties of laws; and so on. Anyone interested in those issues can benefit from some understanding of laws.

There are interesting puzzles about laws themselves:

1. *Metaphysical issues:* What kind of things are laws? Most people believe that laws are different from material entities such as particles and fields, because, for one thing, laws seem to *govern* the material entities. But what is this governing relation? What makes material entities respect such laws?

2. *Epistemological issues:* How do we have epistemic access to laws? Many different candidate laws can yield the same data, a phenomenon known as empirical equivalence. How should we decide which ones to accept? Many people believe that laws apply not just in our local region but everywhere in spacetime. Are we justified in holding such beliefs given our finite and limited evidence?

3. *The marks of the nomic:* There are certain features, such as simplicity, universality, exactness, and objectivity, that we normally associate with laws (the nomic elements of reality). How should we understand those hallmarks, in light of the metaphysics and the epistemology of laws?

Such questions do not have straightforward answers, and they cannot be directly tested in empirical experiments. They fall in the domain of philosophy.

The Great Divide in metaphysical debates about laws is between Humeans, who think that laws are merely descriptions, and non-Humeans, who think

---

[1] I use "fundamental laws," "laws of physics," "physical laws," and "laws" interchangeably unless noted otherwise.

that laws govern.[2] Humeans maintain that laws merely describe how matter is distributed in the universe. In Lewis's version (1973, 1983, 1986), laws are just certain efficient summaries of the distribution of matter in the universe, also known as the *Humean mosaic*, an example of which is a four-dimensional spacetime occupied by particles and fields. All there is in fundamental reality is the Humean mosaic; nothing enforces patterns or moves particles or fields around. On the face of it, Humeanism is highly revisionary; it regards patterns in nature as ultimately unexplained. A common theme in non-Humean views is that laws govern the distribution of matter. By appealing to the governing laws, the patterns are explained. How laws perform such a role is a matter of debate, and there are differences of opinion between reductionist non-Humeans such as Armstrong (1983) and primitivist non-Humeans such as Maudlin (2007).

Many physicists and philosophers have non-Humean sympathies. However, when they first encounter the philosophical literature on laws, they face a dilemma. They reject Humeanism, but they find traditional non-Humeanism unattractive. For example, some accounts explain laws in terms of other entities, such as Platonic universals or Aristotelian dispositions, which are foreign to scientific practice. Other accounts severely limit the forms of laws one is allowed to consider. It is sometimes assumed that the governing view requires that all laws should be *dynamical* laws that *produce* later states of the world from earlier ones, in accord with the direction of time that makes a fundamental distinction between past and future. Call this conception of governing *dynamic production*. However, reflecting on the variety of kinds of laws that physicists present as fundamental, we find many that do not fit in the form of dynamical laws. These include principles of least action (that constrain physical history between two times), the Einstein equation of general relativity (which in its usual presentation is non-dynamical), and the Past Hypothesis (of a low-entropy boundary condition of the universe). Moreover, even when physicists postulate dynamical laws, dynamic production in accord with a fundamental direction of time does not seem essential to how these laws govern the world or explain the observed phenomena. Many physicists and philosophers regard the direction of time as an emergent feature of reality, not something at the fundamental level. Hence, we have good reasons to consider more flexible and minimalist versions of non-Humeanism that better accommodate modern physics.

I present and develop a minimal primitivist view (MinP) about laws of nature, introduced in Chen and Goldstein (2022), that disentangles the governing conception from dynamic production, and requires no reduction or analysis

---

[2] This is an oversimplification as there are some non-Humeans, such as Aristotelian Reductionists, who do not think that laws govern. See Section 4.3.

of laws into something else. It is a non-Humean view where laws govern the universe. On MinP:

- (Primitivism) Fundamental laws are regarded as fundamental facts of the universe; they are not reducible or analyzable into universals, dispositions, or anything else. MinP regards laws as elements of fundamental reality.
- (Minimalism) Fundamental laws govern by constraining the physical possibilities of the entire spacetime and its contents.[3] They need not exclusively be dynamical laws, and their governance does not presuppose a fundamental direction of time.

MinP captures the essence of the governing view without taking on extraneous commitments. Because of the primitivism and the minimalism, MinP accommodates a variety of candidate fundamental laws. The flexibility of MinP is, I believe, a virtue. It is an empirical matter what forms the fundamental laws take on; one's metaphysical theory of laws should be open to accommodating the diverse kinds of laws entertained by physicists. MinP encourages openness.

My goal is to introduce readers to contemporary philosophical issues about laws. I shall focus on MinP, as it provides a unifying lens for thinking about such issues and a clear contrast from traditional accounts. First, various conceptual connections are illustrated, more or less straightforwardly, by thinking about how laws constrain. MinP is a useful entry point into this debate, as one can appreciate the core issues about laws without prior familiarity with deep issues in metaphysics (such as universals, dispositions, and Humean supervenience).

Second, MinP is the ideal non-Humean theory in contrast to Humeanism. We are able to better appreciate their fundamental difference, which is about explanatory priority. The better contrast clarifies the epistemological issues concerning the discovery of physical laws on both Humeanism and non-Humeanism. Our epistemic access to physical laws is based on certain epistemic principles regarding the simplicity and explanatory virtues of physical laws. It turns out that both Humeans and non-Humeans need to posit such epistemic principles in addition to the metaphysical accounts about what laws are.

---

[3] As a first approximation, I assume that spacetime is fundamental. This assumption is not essential to MinP. One can consider non-spatio-temporal worlds governed by minimal primitivist laws. For those worlds, one can understand MinP as suggesting that laws constrain the physical possibilities of the world, whatever non-spatio-temporal structure it may have. Indeed, if one regards time itself as emergent, one may find it natural to understand governing in an atemporal and direction-less sense. I also assume that laws are global entities, governing entire spacetime and its contents, rather than local ones that apply only to subsystems of the universe. For a discussion about the latter perspective and its conceptual implications, see Ismael (2016).

Finally, a clear focus on the epistemic principles allows us to reexamine our commitments to certain hallmarks of physical laws – simplicity, exactness, and objectivity. The metaphysical and epistemological discussions provide principled motivations for whether and how we should associate them with laws.

This Element is intended for advanced undergraduate students, graduate students, and professional researchers in philosophy, physics, and mathematics who are interested in philosophical issues about laws. We will see how to navigate competing concerns to arrive at a particular view about laws and assess it in relation to other accounts. Thus, readers may find in it an illustration of the considerations, concepts, and tools that are presently employed in debates about laws. I will keep technical details at an appropriate level, so that the Element is accessible to those who do not specialize in philosophy of physics.

2 Conceptual Connections

Laws occupy a central place in a systematic philosophical account of the physical world. What makes them interesting is their connections to a wide range of issues, such as ontology, modality, explanations, counterfactuals, causation, time, induction, determinism, chance, and fundamentality. (This section can also serve as a standalone introduction to the conceptual foundations about physical laws that are often implicitly assumed in the philosophical literature.)

2.1 Ontology, Nomology, and Possibility

A well-formulated physical theory contains two parts: (1) a fundamental ontology about what things there are in the physical world, and (2) a fundamental nomology about how such things behave. The two are deeply connected. We focus on (2) in the rest of this Element. Here we say a few words about (1) and how the two are connected.

Let us start with a first-pass definition of the fundamental ontology of a theory:

Fundamental Ontology The fundamental ontology of a physical theory refers to the fundamental material objects, their fundamental properties, and the spacetime they occupy, according to that theory.

For a familiar example, consider a version of Newtonian gravitation theory. Its fundamental ontology has three components:

- Fundamental material objects: N particles
- Fundamental properties: their masses, $(m_1, m_2, \ldots, m_N)$, and their trajectories in physical space, $(q_1(t), q_2(t), \ldots, q_N(t))$

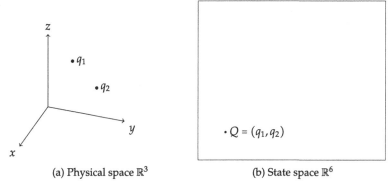

(a) Physical space $\mathbb{R}^3$ (b) State space $\mathbb{R}^6$

Figure 1 Configuration of a two-particle universe, represented in (a) physical space and (b) state space.

- Spacetime: a three-dimensional Euclidean space, represented by the Cartesian coordinate space $\mathbb{R}^3$, and 1-dimensional time, represented by $\mathbb{R}^1$

For simplicity, let us assume that all N particles have equal mass $m = 1$ in the chosen unit. We can define the following concepts:

(i) Physical states. The fundamental physical state of the universe at time t is the instantaneous state of the fundamental ontology at t, which specifies the arrangement of fundamental material objects and their properties at t. In the example of Newtonian gravitation theory, the state of the N-particle universe at time t is a list $(q_1(t), q_2(t), \ldots, q_N(t))$ (see Figure 1(a)), together with the mass values that do not depend on time. Call $Q(t) = (q_1(t), q_2(t), \ldots, q_N(t))$ a *configuration* of the universe.

(It is often useful to consider other information, such as momenta of the N particles, $(p_1(t), p_2(t), \ldots, p_N(t))$, alongside positions. If we understand momenta as velocities (changes in positions) multiplied by mass, then momenta need not be fundamental properties of the particles. A state description with both positions and momenta, $X(t) = (q_1(t), q_2(t), \ldots, q_N(t); p_1(t), p_2(t), \ldots, p_N(t))$, which includes more information than the fundamental physical state, can still be regarded as a physical state.)

(ii) State spaces. There are many possible states for the universe to be at any time. A space of all such possible states is a state space. The space of all possible configurations is called the *configuration space*. Each point in the configuration space corresponds to a possible value of $Q(t)$, a possible list of the positions of N particles in $\mathbb{R}^3$. The configuration space is represented by $\mathbb{R}^{3N}$ (Figure 1(b)).

(When it is useful to consider momenta in addition to particle positions, as in classical mechanics, we may define a space of higher dimensions called the *phase space*. Each point in the phase space corresponds to $X(t)$, a possible list

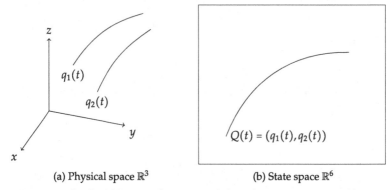

(a) Physical space $\mathbb{R}^3$ (b) State space $\mathbb{R}^6$

Figure 2 Physical history of a two-particle universe, represented in two spaces.

of the positions *and momenta* of N particles in $\mathbb{R}^3$. The list $X(t)$ is twice as long as $Q(t)$. The phase space is represented by $\mathbb{R}^{6N}$.)

(iii) Physical histories. We can regard a physical history of the N-particle universe as a history of its physical states at different times. The most intuitive way is to represent the physical history as N curves in physical space, corresponding to the positions of the N particles at different times (Figure 2(a)). The state spaces provide mathematically convenient but more abstract representations. The physical history of the entire universe corresponds to a single curve in the high-dimensional configuration space, representing the configurations at different times (Figure 2(b)). (It also can be represented as a single curve in phase space.)[4] Notice that the concept of physical histories does not presuppose a direction of time. The arrow-less curves that represent physical histories can be regarded as direction-less histories that do not distinguish between the past and the future. The curves tell us whether state B is temporally between states A and C, but not whether state B is earlier than C.

Next, let us define the fundamental nomology of a theory.

Fundamental Nomology The fundamental nomology of a physical theory refers to the fundamental laws in the physical theory.

The fundamental laws of Newtonian gravitation theory can be represented by the following equations:

- The dynamical law: $F = ma$, or equivalently $F_i(t) = m_i \frac{d^2 q_i(t)}{dt^2}$

---

[4] In the relativistic context, space and time become intertwined in such a way that there is no fundamental notion of physical state at a time. The more fundamental notion is the spacetime histories of N particles. We may represent this as N curves, also called *world lines*, in a four-dimensional spacetime.

- The force law: $F = GMm/r^2$, or equivalently $F_i(t) = -\sum_{j \neq i}^{N} Gm_i m_j \frac{q_i(t) - q_j(t)}{|q_i(t) - q_j(t)|^3}$, with G the gravitational constant

For a Newtonian universe with N particles, these laws tell us which set of physical histories are permissible. We may capture this with a natural interpretation in terms of possible worlds. A possible world is a logically consistent description of spacetime and its contents, namely the distribution of fundamental properties and material objects in spacetime. A possible world can be represented in multiple ways, with N curves in physical space or spacetime, or a single curve in a high-dimensional state space. The collection of all such worlds permitted by physical laws forms the set of nomological possibilities.

More precisely, a nomologically possible world of theory T is a logically consistent description of spacetime and its contents such that (1) the fundamental objects and properties are restricted to those kinds mentioned by the fundamental laws in T, and (2) their arrangement is compatible with those laws. In other words, a nomologically possible world of theory T is a model of the laws of T. This definition can be specialized to the actual physical laws. The actual world is a very special one – the spacetime with the actual arrangement of objects and their properties. We define the following:

- A possible world w: a spacetime and a distribution of material contents.[5]
- The actual world α: the actual spacetime and the actual distribution of material contents.
- Material contents: material objects and their qualitative properties.
- Ω^T: the set of possible worlds that satisfy the fundamental laws specified in theory T.
- Ω_α: the set of possible worlds that satisfy the actual fundamental laws of α, that is the set of all nomologically possible worlds.

Note that $\Omega_\alpha = \Omega^T$ only when T is the actual theory of the world, that is the axioms of T correspond to the fundamental laws governing α. As a conceptual truth, we also have that $\alpha \in \Omega_\alpha$.

The definitions are global in character, as they concern entire possible worlds. Sometimes we are also interested in parts of worlds, such as whether certain events of a 30-minute interval is nomologically possible or impossible. We may define the following:

---

[5] For simplicity, I assume that possible worlds have a fundamental spatio-temporal structure. See also footnote 3.

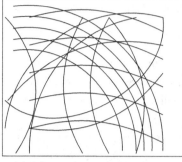 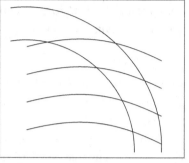

(a) Arbitrary histories in state space (b) Nomologically possible histories

Figure 3 Laws select a special subclass of physical histories as the nomologically possible histories.

Nomological Possibility A sequence of events is nomologically possible if and only if it occurs in some nomologically possible world.

Nomological Necessity A sequence of events is nomologically necessary if and only if it occurs in every nomologically possible world.

We may think of a choice of a fundamental ontology as pinning down abstract *state spaces* that tell us what kind of physical states are available. But it does not pin down which histories in those state spaces are nomologically possible (Figure 3(a)). The choice of a fundamental nomology selects a special subclass of histories corresponding to the nomologically possible ones which are also called physical possibilities (Figure 3(b)).

2.2 Counterfactuals and Causation

Laws *support* counterfactuals.[6] A counterfactual is a conditional of the form "if A were the case, then B would be the case." (We often focus only on those for which A does not occur.) In a counterfactual, the consequence does not follow from the antecedent as a matter of logic; they are joined together by laws. For example, consider:

C1 If this match had been struck, it would have lit.

C2 If this match had been struck, it would not have lit.

Suppose C1 is true and C2 false. For either one, the consequent and its negation are logically compatible with the antecedent. Hence, it is not logic alone

---

[6] In Section 4.4, we discuss Lange's view according to which counterfactuals ground laws.

that renders C1 true and C2 false. What nonlogical fact is needed? Many agree that it involves some laws. But why laws in particular, but not just general facts of the form "every match that is struck in oxygen rich, dry, and no-wind condition is lit?" Generality is not sufficient, and lawfulness is crucial. Suppose every coin in my pocket is silver. Nevertheless, the following counterfactual is false:

C3 If this coin were in my pocket, it would have been silver.

The problem is that the general fact *every coin in my pocket is silver* is accidental. To support a counterfactual, the nonlogical fact needs to have nomological necessity, corresponding to a law. To see this more clearly, consider counterfactuals about physical systems:

C4 If this ice cube were placed in a cup of hot tea, it would melt 30 seconds later.

C5 If there were one more planet orbiting around the sun, it would have an elliptical orbit.

C6 If the polarizer were oriented at 30 degrees from the median line, 25 percent of the pairs of photons would pass.

To evaluate such counterfactuals, we need knowledge of the relevant laws (in thermodynamics, classical mechanics, and quantum mechanics). For C4, we can consider the nomologically possible worlds where this ice cube were placed in a cup of hot tea, and check whether the ice cube is melted 30 seconds later in all (or most) of them. If the answer the yes, then C4 is true. For C5, we consider the nomologically possible worlds with a ninth planet orbiting around the sun and check whether it has an elliptical orbit. And so on. There are conceptual nuances and technical challenges in spelling out the exact nomic algorithms for evaluating such counterfactuals. (For a range of different proposals, see Lewis (1979), Albert (2000, 2015), Kutach (2002) and Loewer (2007a). For an updated discussion, see Fernandes (2023).)

Counterfactuals are related to deliberation, influence, and control. Rational deliberation depends on evaluating counterfactuals with various different suppositions, representing different options, and assessing their outcomes. If action A were selected, outcome O would result. If counterfactuals have nomic involvement, then so are those notions. Knowledge about counterfactuals is practically relevant.

Counterfactuals are often linked to causation. An influential approach seeks to analyze causation in terms of counterfactual dependence. Roughly speaking, event A causes event E if and only if the following two counterfactuals are true:

C7 If A were the case, then C would be the case.

C8 If A were not the case, then C would not be the case.

For example, Suzy throws a rock at a window and the window breaks. Her throw causes the breaking of the window, because if she had not thrown the rock at the window it would not have broken. Due to various counterexamples to such an account, many people have given up the project of *analyzing* causation in terms of counterfactual dependence. Nevertheless, counterfactual dependence seems to capture an important aspect of causation. The central idea is also preserved in contemporary structural equation models of causation. For more on the latter, see Hitchcock (2023).

2.3 Dynamic Production and the Direction of Time

A concept closely related to causation is that of dynamic production. It is the idea that events in the past, together with the laws, bring about events in the future. (For a comparison of production and counterfactual dependence, see Hall (2004).) For some people, dynamic production is constitutive of how laws govern and explain. Laws govern the universe by dynamically producing the subsequent states from earlier ones; an event is explained by appealing to the laws and the prior events that produce it.

The emphasis on dynamic production is often associated with an emphasis on dynamical laws and the direction of time. If dynamic production is how laws govern, laws should presumably be dynamical laws that evolve the states of the universe successively in time. They should be exclusively what Maudlin (2007) calls *Fundamental Laws of Temporal Evolution* (FLOTEs). Examples of FLOTEs include Newton's $F = ma$, Schrödinger's equation, and Dirac's equation, but not Einstein's equation, Gauss's law, or boundary-condition laws. Moreover, for dynamic production to make sense, the temporal development should be directed only from the past to the future. However, the laws in modern physics are blind to the past-future distinction; they are (essentially) time-reversal invariant in the sense that for any nomologically possible history going in one temporal direction, its temporal reverse is also nomologically possible. Where does the direction of time come from? A natural idea, on this picture, is to make the direction of time a fundamental feature of the universe.

We may summarize this package of ideas as (1) a restriction of the form of laws:

Only FLOTEs The only kind of fundamental laws are fundamental laws of temporal evolution (FLOTEs).

(2) a commitment to dynamic production as for how laws explain:

Dynamic Production Laws explain by producing later states of the universe from earlier ones.

and (3) a metaphysical posit about the direction of time:

Temporal Direction Primitivism The direction of time is a fundamental feature of the universe.

Many people accept the package because it seems intuitive. Some build it into their theories of lawhood. An example is Maudlin (2007), who expresses these ideas eloquently:

> The universe started out in some particular initial state. The laws of temporal evolution operate, whether deterministically or stochastically, from that initial state to generate or produce later states. (p.174)
>
> This sort of explanation takes the term initial quite seriously: the initial state temporally precedes the explananda, which can be seen to arise from it (by means of the operation of the law). (p.176)
>
> The universe, as well as all the smaller parts of it, is made: it is an ongoing enterprise, generated from a beginning and guided towards its future by physical law. (p.182)

Despite the intuitive picture, in my view dynamic production is inadequate for modern physics. It may be a useful heuristic picture to start out with, but once we see more examples of candidate laws and appreciate the explanations they provide, it is natural to replace the picture with something more flexible (allowing non-FLOTEs to be laws) and without a commitment to dynamic production or a fundamental direction of time.

An alternative approach, which I favor, is to understand the direction of time and dynamic production as important but derivative features of the physical world, partly explained by a boundary-condition law called the *Past Hypothesis*. On this approach, the direction of time is understood in terms of an entropy gradient that arises from a new law – at one temporal boundary, the universe is in a low-entropy state. Given the Past Hypothesis as a nomic constraint, it is plausible to expect that most solutions to the dynamical equations will be ones that relax toward the thermodynamic equilibrium (maximum entropy) in the direction away from the temporal boundary where the Past Hypothesis applies.

Hence, almost all the nomological possible worlds are such that they will display an entropy gradient, giving rise to an emergent (nonfundamental) direction of time. It has been argued that it is compatible with the Humean approach of laws, but it is also compatible with non-Humeanism. On the non-Humean account I introduce in Section 3, laws explain, not by producing the states of the universe in time, but by constraining physical possibilities. Dynamic production may also be regarded as a derivative concept.

Allowing non-FLOTEs to be laws, the alternative approach opens up many new possibilities. Still, we may sometimes prefer FLOTEs, but the preferences are not grounded in metaphysical prohibitions about the forms of laws, but in methodological and epistemic reasons that certain dynamical laws offer simple and compelling explanations of observed phenomena. As I shall argue, the alternative approach is better suited for accommodating the variety of kinds of laws in modern physics and understanding the explanations they provide.

2.4 Determinism and Chance

Determinism and indeterminism are properties of laws. In his survey article, Hoefer (2016) provides the following (first-pass) characterization of determinism (emphases original):

Determinism$_0$ The *world* is *governed by* (or is *under the sway of*) determinism if and only if, given a specified *way things are at a time t*, the way things go *thereafter* is fixed as a matter of *natural law*.

As Hoefer notes, the word "thereafter" suggests that determinism in this sense is future-directed but not past-directed.

The core idea about determinism can be captured with nomological possibilities and without appealing to a direction of time. Borrowing ideas from (Montague 1974, pp.319–321), (Lewis 1983, p.360), and (Earman 1986, pp.12–13), I define determinism as follows (also see Figure 4):

Determinism$_T$ Theory T is *deterministic* just in case, for any two $w, w' \in \Omega^T$, if w and w' agree at any time, they agree at all times.

Determinism$_\alpha$ The actual world α is *deterministic* just in case, for any two $w, w' \in \Omega_\alpha$, if w and w' agree at any time, they agree at all times.

Determinism is true just in case α is deterministic. My definitions correspond to what Earman (1986, p.13) calls *Laplacian determinism*. The basic idea is that the nomologically possible worlds never cross in state space (like Figure 4 and

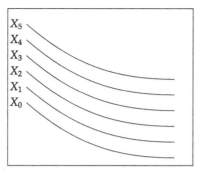

X_5
X_4
X_3
X_2
X_1
X_0

Figure 4 Schematic illustration of a deterministic theory T. Ω^T contains six nomologically possible worlds that do not cross in state space.

unlike Figure 3(b)). By using four-dimensional spacetimes, such definitions are more suitable for relativistic contexts as well as worlds without a fundamental direction of time.

Indeterminism is true just in case determinism is false. When a theory is indeterministic, it may also posit objective probabilities, some of which play roles similar to those of physical chances. There is an interesting question whether chance can coexist with determinism. In classical and quantum statistical mechanics, even when the dynamical laws are deterministic, we may still posit probabilistic boundary conditions over nomologically possible initial states of the universe. Ismael (2009) has argued that they are indispensable for the predictive and explanatory success of those theories. Barrett (1995) suggests that the probabilistic boundary conditions, in theories like Bohmian mechanics, are as important for the empirical adequacy of the theory as the dynamical equations. For a survey about deterministic chances, see Hoefer (2016, sect. 5).

We can define a stronger variety of determinism called *strong determinism*. According to Penrose (1989), strong determinism is "not just a matter of the future being determined by the past; the *entire history of the universe is fixed*, according to some precise mathematical scheme, for all time" (emphasis original, p.432). While Penrose defines strong determinism in terms of *mathematical schemes*, I propose to define it in terms of *fundamental laws*: a strongly deterministic theory of physics is one that, according to its fundamental laws, permits exactly one nomologically possible world; our world is strongly deterministic just in case it is the only nomologically possible world (see also Figure 5):

Strong Determinism$_T$ Theory T is strongly deterministic if $|\Omega^T| = 1$, that is its fundamental laws are compatible with exactly one possible world.

Strong Determinism$_\alpha$ The actual world α is strongly deterministic if $\Omega_\alpha = \{\alpha\}$.

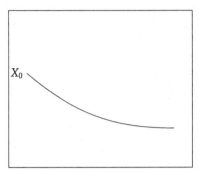

Figure 5 Schematic illustration of a strongly deterministic theory T. Ω^T contains exactly one nomologically possible world.

Under my definitions, strong determinism is stronger than determinism in a precise sense: whenever the definition of determinism is applicable, strong determinism logically implies determinism but not vice versa.

Strong determinism is more general than determinism. There are circumstances where strong determinism applies but determinism does not (at least not naturally). That is because defining strong determinism only requires the minimal notion of the cardinality of the set of models, while defining determinism requires a notion of temporal agreement, which is not always guaranteed. For example, we can contemplate worlds without a fundamental spatiotemporal structure (such as those without metrical or topological time) of which there may not be natural extension of determinism. We may not be able to say whether such worlds are deterministic, for the concept simply does not apply. But even if w is such a world, we can still assess the cardinality of Ω_w, the set of models compatible with the fundamental laws that govern w. $|\Omega_w|$ is either 1 or larger than 1. Hence, the entailment relation discussed in the last paragraph is valid only when the proviso holds – whenever determinism is applicable.

There are many interesting works on free will, rational deliberation, and agency under determinism. For some examples, see Hoefer (2002), Ismael (2016), and Loewer (2020a). Strong determinism has not received much attention in the philosophical literature until recently. See Chen (2021b, 2022c, 2023b) and Adlam (2022a). Several proposed theories of quantum cosmology aspire to be strongly deterministic. See Hartle and Hawking (1983) and Page (2009). Strong determinism is a possible feature of our physical theory, but Hartle (1996, 1997) goes further and suggests that it is a requirement.

2.5 Prediction and Explanation

To make predictions about the future, or retrodictions about the past, we rely on laws. For example, to predict the positions of planets in the solar system (relative to the sun), we need their current configuration plus laws of Newtonian gravitation theory to calculate their subsequent positions. We can also use the same laws to retrodict the positions of those planets in the last millions of years. Predictions and retrodictions are enabled by physical laws.

Laws are connected to scientific explanations. The search for physical laws is motivated by various "Why" questions. Why do apples fall at this rate from this height? Why do planets move in such orbits? Why do ice cubes melt in a cup of hot tea? Laws provide answers to such questions.

There is no sharp line between explanations and predictions (or retrodictions), as they often overlap. When there is an accurate prediction based on laws, there is often a corresponding explanation enabled by laws. However, they can come apart. Some laws provide accurate predictions but no satisfying explanation. For example, in orthodox quantum mechanics, we have a practical algorithm that makes successful predictions. The algorithm associates abstract mathematical objects on Hilbert space to experimental setups and yields predictions about measurement outcomes. Those postulates may be regarded as laws of orthodox quantum mechanics. They are, however, terrible candidates for laws, for they are disunified and not appropriately linked to a fundamental physical ontology. It would be far better to replace them with a simpler and more unified set of laws, explicitly defined over some fundamental physical states, from which those measurement postulates can be derived as theorems. Hence, solutions to the quantum measurement problem (see Myrvold (2017) and Maudlin (2019) for reviews) can be seen as providing better and more satisfying explanations. (Readers familiar with the recent discussion about 'explainable' artificial intelligence (AI) may see a parallel.)

Let us connect prediction and explanation with the previous discussion about determinism and strong determinism. We can distinguish different kinds of prediction and explanation. On determinism, we have conditional predictions:

Conditional Prediction Conditional on the state of the universe at some time (or states of the universe at some finite interval of time), one can in-principle deduce, using the fundamental laws, the state of the universe at any time.

In contrast, strong determinism enables what I call *strong prediction*:

Strong Prediction One can in-principle deduce, using the fundamental laws alone, the state of the universe at any time.

Similarly, deterministic laws account for a general temporal pattern (cf. Russell (1913)):

Conditional Explanation Conditional on the state of the universe at some time (or states of the universe at some finite interval of time), one can explain, using the fundamental laws, the state of the universe at any time.

Strongly deterministic laws can explain more. They underwrite conditional explanations but also account for unconditional facts:

Strong Explanation One can explain, using the fundamental laws alone, the state of the universe at any time.

We may understand both types of explanations in the deductive-nomological (DN) model. On this approach, a scientific explanation contains two parts: an *explanandum* describing the phenomenon to be explained, and an *explanans* that account for the phenomenon. There are two requirements for a successful DN explanation. First, the explanation from the explanans to the explanandum should take the form of a deductive argument. Second, the explanans must involve, as premises for the deductive argument, at least one law of nature. As an example, consider the explanation of the orbit of Earth around the sun via Newtonian mechanics. The explanandum is the orbit. The explanans includes facts about the mass of the Earth, the mass of the Sun, Newton's law of universal gravitation, and Newton's laws of motion. The exact orbit follows, as a mathematical solution, from the laws plus initial condition of the positions and velocities of massive objects. In the DN model, a conditional explanation is one that involves at least one law and at least one non-law as the explanans; a strong explanation is one where laws are the only explanans.

Philosophers have raised many objections to the DN model as a universal model of scientific explanation (Woodward and Ross 2021, Sect. 2). However, the DN model is a simple and fruitful approach to think about explanations in physics. A difficulty of applying the DN model lies in the fact that we lack criteria to distinguish laws from non-laws. The problem is not unique to the DN model, as competing accounts of scientific explanation often invoke concepts connected to laws, such as causation.[7] Hence, the task of coming up with a satisfactory account of explanation in physics is bound up with the task of coming up with a satisfactory account of laws. Insofar as simplicity is an important feature of laws, it may be essential to explanations as well. How exactly simplicity is connected to laws, and how it figures in explanations, is a topic we will return in Sections 3–5.

---

[7] I thank Tyler Hildebrand for the suggestion.

2.6 Problems of Induction

Induction is the inference from observed phenomena to unobserved ones. It is essential to the scientific enterprise, but difficult to justify. There are two problems of induction widely discussed in the philosophical literature: Hume's problem and Goodman's problem (see Henderson (2022) for a review). Both can be understood in relation to laws.

Hume asks us to consider what justifies the inference from

I1 All observed instances of bread of a particular appearance have been nourishing.

to

I2 The next instance of bread of that appearance will be nourishing.

We often appeal to a Principle of Uniformity:

PU Nature is uniform.

This is intended to explain why events in nature continue the same way, why past and future are relevantly similar, and why the next instance of bread of that type will also be nourishing. A major difficulty that Hume has identified is that we do not have noncircular justifications for inductive inference, because our justification for PU comes from induction.

Many of us accept the rationality of induction. One might take the lesson of Hume's argument to be that we should make a substantive assumption about the world as the basis for inductive inference. PU is a good candidate and should be taken as epistemically fundamental that is not justified by anything else.

However, Goodman's "new riddle of induction" shows that even PU is insufficient. Suppose, up to time t, all observed emeralds are green. Two interpretations of PU will give us divergent predictions. Under the assumption that, in nature, color distributions in terms of *green* and *blue* continue over time, then we infer that all emeralds are green and the emerald observed after t will be green. However, we can also understand uniformity in terms of the temporal distribution of *grue* and *bleen*, where *grue* means green and observed before t and blue and observed at or after t. Under the second interpretation of PU, we should infer that all emeralds are grue and the emerald observed after t will be blue. This can also be generalized to more realistic predicates used in physics.

Some respond by suggesting we need a specific version of PU. It should license normal inductive inferences but not "gruesome" ones. Consider:

PU+ Nature is uniform for phenomena described in natural predicates.

On PU+, we stipulate that the pattern of green and blue continues over time. This supports the inductive generalization that future observed emeralds are green, and does not support the hypothesis that they are blue.

However, PU and its more specific version PU+ face more fundamental problems. Specified in fundamental / natural predicates, nature is not uniform. Moreover, the uniformity of nature is not necessary for induction.

The mosaic we inhabit, described in terms of the matter distribution in space-time, is manifestly non-uniform. We do not live in an empty universe that is completely homogeneous and isotropic, exactly the same in all regions and directions. The spacetime region we occupy is quite different from regions with violent collisions of stars and merging of black holes. What happens on earth differs from even a nearby patch – the core of the sun, where nuclear fusion converts hydrogen into helium. The variety and complexity in the matter distribution does not diminish our confidence in the viability and the success of induction. In fact, nonuniformity of a certain kind is arguably necessary for the observed temporal asymmetries in our universe, which may be a precondition for induction.[8]

Suppose we replace PU+ with the principle that we should expect that the law L be uniform. This principle, with a focus on the law instead of the mosaic, is in the right direction, but it still has problems. Suppose we understand the uniformity of L to mean that it is of the form "for all x, if Fx then Gx," which is a regularity, that is a universally quantified statement about the mosaic, holding for everything, everywhere, and everywhen. The principle becomes vacuous, as any statement can be translated into a universally quantified sentence. That I have five coins in my pocket is equivalent to the statement that, for everything and everywhere and everywhen, I have five coins in my pocket. Suppose we understand the uniformity of L to mean that it does not refer to any particular individual, location, or time. The principle becomes too restrictive. There are candidate laws that do refer to particular facts, such as the Past Hypothesis of statistical mechanics, quantum equilibrium distribution in Bohmian mechanics, the Weyl curvature hypothesis in general relativity, and the No-Boundary Wave Function proposal in quantum cosmology (see Section 3.3). These laws can be accepted on scientific and inductive grounds, and may be required to ultimately vindicate our inductive practice. Suppose we understand it to mean that the same law applies everywhere in spacetime. The principle again becomes vacuous, as even an intuitively nonuniform law, unfriendly to induction, can be described by a uniform law with a temporal variation, such as

---

[8] See Albert (2000). See Wallace (2010) and Rovelli (2019) for the importance of the hydrogen-helium imbalance in the early universe to the existence of the relevant time asymmetries.

$$F = ma \text{ for } (-\infty, t] \text{ and } F = \left(8m^9 - \frac{1}{7}m^5 + \pi m^3 + km^2 + m\right) a \text{ for } (t, \infty)$$

(1)

The same law can be applied to everywhere in spacetime.

As I suggest in Section 5, what induction ultimately requires is the reasonable simplicity of laws (expressed in natural predicates and traded off with other explanatory virtues).

2.7 Fundamentality

The final issue concerns fundamentality. In metaphysics, there is much discussion about fundamental ontology (e.g. particles, fields, and spacetime) and nonfundamental ontology (e.g. tables, cats, and galaxies). There is also a distinction between fundamental laws and nonfundamental laws. How should they be distinguished?

Consider the following definition of fundamental laws:

Fundamental Laws For any world *w*, fundamental laws of nature in *w* are the nonmathematical axioms (basic postulates) of the complete fundamental physical theory of *w*.

For a physical theory to be complete in world *w*, it needs to entail all the important regularities in *w*, including those described by nonfundamental laws (such as laws of chemistry, biology, and so on). For a physical theory to be fundamental in *w*, it cannot be derived from another nonequivalent physical theory that is true in *w*. Hence, in a quantum world, classical mechanics is not a fundamental theory, because it can be derived from quantum mechanics (via approximations in some limit). However, in a classical world, classical mechanics is a fundamental theory because quantum mechanics is not true in such a world. The physical theory can employ some mathematics, but the mathematical axioms are not laws of nature. Hence, the fundamental laws of nature are the *nonmathematical axioms*.

Laws in *w* are either fundamental or nonfundamental in *w*. I require nonfundamental laws in *w* be derivable[9] from fundamental laws in *w*. But not all deductive consequences of fundamental laws are laws, for otherwise we could trivialize the notion of laws by using disjunction introduction. Some deductive consequences will be more important than others because they support counterfactuals and are extraordinarily useful and simple. Identifying the

---

[9] The relevant derivations may also involve approximations and idealizations.

sufficient conditions for nonfundamental laws is an important project, but I do not pursue it here. Instead, I suggest a necessary condition for a law to be nonfundamental in w:

Necessary Condition for Nonfundamental Laws In any world w, if a law of nature is a nonfundamental law in w, then it can be derived from the fundamental laws in w.[10]

Consequently, a law that cannot be so derived in w is a fundamental law in w. An example of a nonfundamental law in our world is the ideal gas law $PV = nRT$ that can be derived from the microphysics. Not all nonfundamental laws have been successfully derived from the fundamental axioms in physics, but what matters is that they can be.

In philosophy of physics, there are debates about the theoretical structure of quantum field theories, a theory that is remarkably accurate for certain predictions about the subatomic particles but employs methods and principles (such as the renormalization technique) not straightforwardly interpretable as fundamental laws. Those debates may give us a richer understanding of how fundamental laws relate to nonfundamental laws. For recent discussions about these issues in relation to fundamentality, see McKenzie (2022) and Williams (2023).

What about fundamental laws themselves? Are they metaphysically fundamental? Or are they metaphysically explained by something else? We turn to these questions in the next section.

2.8 Summary

The conceptual connections discussed above are evidence of the centrality of laws in a comprehensive philosophy of science. As a first step toward such a philosophy, one needs to develop a metaphysical account of what laws are.

3 Minimal Primitivism

As an example of a metaphysical account of laws, I introduce the view about laws that Sheldon Goldstein and I call *Minimal Primitivism* (MinP). It provides a unifying lens for viewing the conceptual connections (Section 2) and a useful starting point for discussing other accounts (Section 4).

---

[10] For people who worry that this principle is too strong, they may restrict it to nonfundamental laws in the domain of physics. Thanks to Tyler Hildebrand for the suggestion.

3.1 Minimal Primitivism (MinP)

According to MinP, fundamental laws are metaphysically fundamental. They do not require anything else to exist. For laws to govern, they are not required to dynamically produce or generate later states of the universe from earlier ones, nor are they required to presume a fundamental direction of time. On MinP, laws govern by constraining the physical possibilities (nomological possibilities). MinP is flexible regarding the form of laws. To summarize, the first part of the view is a metaphysical thesis:

Minimal Primitivism Fundamental laws of nature are certain primitive facts about the world. There is no restriction on the form of the fundamental laws. They govern the behavior of material objects by constraining the physical possibilities.

Even though there is no metaphysical restriction on the form of fundamental laws, it is rational to expect them to have certain nice features, such as simplicity and informativeness. On Humean Reductionism (Section 4.1), those features are metaphysically constitutive of laws, but on MinP they are merely epistemic guides for discovering and evaluating the laws. At the end of the day, they are defeasible guides, and we can arrive at the wrong laws even if we are fully rational in scientific investigations. The second part of our view is an epistemic thesis:

Epistemic Guides Even though theoretical virtues such as simplicity, informativeness, fit, and degree of naturalness are not metaphysically constitutive of fundamental laws, they are good epistemic guides for discovering and evaluating them.

Let me offer some clarifications:

(i) *Primitive Facts.* Fundamental laws of nature are certain primitive facts about the world, in the sense that they are not metaphysically dependent on, reducible to, or analyzable in terms of anything else. If the concrete physical reality corresponds to a Humean mosaic, then fundamental laws are facts that transcend the mosaic. Many physicists may even regard fundamental laws as more important than the mosaic itself. Depending on one's metaphysical attitude toward mathematics and logic, there might be mathematical and logical facts that are also primitive in that sense. For example, arithmetical facts such as $2 + 3 = 5$ and the logical law of excluded middle may also be primitive facts that transcend the concrete physical reality and constrain the physical possibilities, since every physical possibility must conform to them. However, we do not think that fundamental laws of nature are purely mathematical or logical. Hence, fundamental laws of nature are not those kinds of primitive facts.[11]

(ii) *The Governing Relation.* On MinP, laws govern by constraining the world (the entire spacetime and its contents). We may understand constraining as a *primitive relation* between fundamental laws and the actual world. We can better understand constraining by drawing conceptual connections to physical possibilities. Laws constrain the world by limiting physical possibilities, of which the actual world is a member. In other words, the actual world is constrained to be compatible with the laws. To use an earlier example, $F = ma$ governs by constraining the physical possibilities to exactly those that are compatible with $F = ma$. If $F = ma$ is a law that governs the actual world, then the actual world is a possibility compatible with $F = ma$.

Constraint differs from dynamic production; it does not require a fundamental distinction between past and future, or one between earlier states and later states. What the laws constrain is the entire spacetime and its contents. In some cases, the constraint imposed by a law can be expressed in terms of differential equations that may be interpreted as determining future states from past ones. (But *not all constraints need be like that.* I discuss some examples in Sections 3.2 and 3.3.)

For a concrete example, consider Hamilton's equations of motion for N point particles with Newtonian masses $(m_1, \ldots, m_N)$ moving in a three-dimensional Euclidean space, whose positions and momenta are $(q_1, \ldots, q_N; p_1, \ldots, p_N)$:

$$\frac{dq_i(t)}{dt} = \frac{\partial H}{\partial p_i}, \quad \frac{dp_i(t)}{dt} = -\frac{\partial H}{\partial q_i}, \tag{2}$$

where $H = H(q_1, \ldots, q_N; p_1, \ldots, p_N)$ is specified in accord with Newtonian gravitation:

$$H = \sum_i^N \frac{p_i^2}{2m_i} - \sum_{1 \leq j < k \leq N} \frac{Gm_j m_k}{|q_j - q_k|}. \tag{3}$$

Suppose Equations (2) and (3) are the fundamental laws that govern our world α. Let Ω^H denote the set of solutions to (2) and (3). Represented geometrically, Ω^H corresponds to a special set of curves on the state space of the N-particle system – the phase space represented by $\mathbb{R}^{6N}$. Saying that (2) and (3) govern our world implies that α should be compatible with them. In other words, Ω^H delineates the set of physical possibilities, and $\alpha \in \Omega^H$.

In this example, the dynamical equations are time-reversible. For every solution in Ω^H, its time reversal under $t \to -t$ and $p \to -p$ is also a solution in Ω^H.

---

[11] A Humean may worry about the intelligibility of those non-Humean primitives. See Hildebrand (2022, Sect. 5) for a discussion about related worries and potential responses.

Since the concept of governing in MinP does not presuppose a fundamental direction of time, two solutions that are time-reversal of each other *can* be identified as the same physical possibility. (If one prefers the representation where the set of physical possibilities contains each possibility exactly once, one can derive a quotient set Ω_α^* from Ω_α with the equivalence relation given by the time-reversal map.)

(iii) *Nomic Equivalence.* We should not think that, in every case, a law is equivalent to the set of possibilities it generates. The two can be different. For example, there are many principles and equations that can give rise to the same set of possibilities denoted by Ω^H. But we expect laws to be simple. One way to pick out the set Ω^H is by giving a complete (and infinitely) long list of possible histories contained in Ω^H. Another is by writing down simple equations, such as (2) and (3), which express simple laws. Hence, the equivalence of laws is not just the equivalence of their classes of models. For two laws to be equivalent, it will require something more.

It is an interesting and open question, on MinP, what more is required and how to understand the equivalence of laws. It seems to me that their equivalence must be related to simplicity and explanations, because a central role for laws to play is to provide an illuminating account of natural phenomena (see Section 3.2). A natural idea, then, is to say that nomic equivalence requires explanatory equivalence, for which simplicity is an important factor. Hence, two fundamental facts that differ in their relative complexity cannot express the same law. (For a survey of the related topic of theoretical equivalence, see Weatherall (2019a, b).)

(iv) *The Mystery Objection.* Some might object that our notion of governing is entirely mysterious (Beebee 2000). The notion of governing seems derived from the notion of government and the notion of being governed. But laws of nature are obviously not imposed by human (or divine) agents. So isn't it mysterious that laws can govern? To that we reply that a better analogy for governing laws is not to human government, but to laws of mathematics and logic. Arithmetical truths such as $2 + 3 = 5$ and logical truths such as the law of excluded middle can also be said to constrain our world. That is, the actual world cannot be a world that violates those mathematical or logical truths. In fact, every possible world needs to respect those truths. In a similar way, laws of physics constrain our world. The actual world cannot be a world that violates the physical laws, and every physically possible world needs to respect those laws. Those modal claims reflect physical laws and mathematical laws. We can also make sense of the difference in scope between those laws. Mathematical laws are more general than physical laws, in the sense that the former are compatible with "more models" than the latter. In any case, mathematical laws and logical laws can also be said to govern the universe in the sense of imposing formal constraints. They generate a class of models and constrain the actual world to be one among them. There is also a difference in epistemic access. In some sense, we discover mathematical and logical laws *a priori*, without the need for experiments or observations, but we discover physical laws *a posteriori*, empirically.

We do not claim that the analogy with mathematical and logical laws completely eliminates the mystery of how physical laws govern. However, we think it dispels the objection as previously stated, in terms of how something can govern the world without being imposed by an agent. If there is more to the mystery objection, it needs to be stated differently. On MinP, laws govern by constraining, and constraining is what they do. This provides the *oomph* behind scientific explanations. (We return to this shortly.) However, in contrast to other non-Humean accounts, such an *oomph* is minimalist. It does not require dynamic production, and it does not require an extra process supplied by a mechanism or an agent.

(v) *Epistemic Guides*. On MinP, even though theoretical virtues are not metaphysically constitutive of lawhood, they are nonetheless excellent epistemic guides for discovering and evaluating them.

Regarding Epistemic Guides, one might ask why those theoretical virtues are reliable guides for finding and evaluating laws. This is a subtle issue, one related to the problems of induction. Unlike Humeans, we cannot appeal to a reductive analysis of laws. (Humeans face a similar issue, as their account raises the worry as to why the fundamental Humean mosaic is so nice that it can be summarized in a simple way after all. Humean supervenience does not by itself solve the problems of induction. See Section 5.) We can offer an empirical justification: the scientific methodology works. In so far as those theoretical virtues are central to scientific methodology, they are good guides for discovering and evaluating laws, and we expect them to continue to work. Can they fail to deliver us the true laws? That is a possibility. However, if the true fundamental laws are complicated and messy, scientists would not be inclined to call them laws.

(vi) *Temporal Variations of the Laws*. According to MinP, can laws change with time? In particular, can fundamental laws be time dependent in such a way that different cosmic epochs are governed by different laws? In principle, MinP allows that possibility. If there is scientific motivation to develop theories in which laws take on different forms at different times, that is sufficient reason to consider a set of laws that govern different times, or a single law that varies in form with time. As a toy example, if we have empirical or theoretical reasons to think that the laws of motion are different on the two sides of the Big Crunch, say Newtonian mechanics and Bohmian mechanics, then different sides of the Crunch can be governed by different laws, or by a single law with a temporal variation. Similarly, MinP is compatible with fundamental constants of nature that have spatial or temporal variations (Dirac (1937); see Uzan (2011) for a review). Hence, on MinP, time-translation invariance may fail even for fundamental laws. Why then should we expect laws to be "uniform" in time so that they are friendly to induction? This is an instance of the previous point (v), to which I return in Section 5.

(vii) *Fundamental vs. Non-fundamental Properties.* According to MinP, can fundamental laws refer to non-fundamental properties, such as entropy or temperature? Many fundamental laws we put forward refer only to fundamental properties. But it is reasonable to consider candidate fundamental laws that refer to nonfundamental properties. Epistemic Guides allows for this, as long as the nonfundamental properties are not too unnatural (all things considered). In the case of the Past Hypothesis, for example, we may sacrifice fundamentality of the property involved but gain a lot of informativeness and simplicity if we invoke the property of entropy. The version of the Past Hypothesis that refers to entropy can still govern by constraining the physical possibilities. (Another strategy is to revise our definition of fundamental property such that any property mentioned by a fundamental law is regarded as fundamental, although it may be analyzable in terms of other fundamental properties. However, this may present a problem for certain views of fundamentality.)

(viii) *Fundamental vs. Non-fundamental Laws.* According to MinP, how are fundamental laws distinguished from nonfundamental laws? MinP allows for a reductionist picture where nonfundamental laws, when properly understood, are reducible to fundamental laws. We can distinguish them in terms of derivability: non-fundamental laws can be (nontrivially) derived from fundamental laws (Section 2.7). For example, the ideal gas law is less fundamental than Newton's laws of motion, in the sense that the ideal gas law can be derived from them in suitable regime. However, derivability may not be sufficient for nonfundamental *lawhood*, as other factors, such as counterfactual and explanatory robustness, may also be relevant.

(ix) *Related Views.* Adlam (2022b) independently proposes an account that is, in certain aspects, similar to MinP; she also suggests we take seriously laws that do not have a time-evolution form. However, her account is not committed to primitivism and seems more at home in a structural realist framework. Meacham (2023)'s nomic-likelihood account is also similar to MinP but Meacham takes objective probabilities as the starting point. Carroll (1994) is often called a primitivist about laws, though recently Carroll (2018) distances his view from primitivism and suggests a non-Humean reductive analysis of laws in terms of causation. Bhogal (2017) proposes a "minimal anti-Humeanism" on which laws are ungrounded (true) universal generalizations. It is compatible with primitivism, but it is less minimalist than MinP. For example, on Bhogal's view, laws cannot be singular facts about particular times or places. However, Bhogal (p.447, fn.1) seems open to relax the requirement that laws have to be universal generalizations. It would be interesting to see how to extend Bhogal's view to do so. Hildebrand and Metcalf (2021) consider a theistic non-Humean account according to laws are created by a supernatural being. Their account is presumably as flexible as MinP, since they do not restrict the forms of laws (unlike Foster (2004)).

3.2 Explanation by Simple Constraint

On MinP, laws explain, but not by accounting for the *dynamic production* of successive states of the universe from earlier ones. They explain by expressing a hidden simplicity, given by compelling constraints that lie beneath complex phenomena. A fundamental direction of time is not required for our notion of explanation.[12]

In a world governed by Newtonian mechanics, particles travel along often complicated trajectories because that is implied by the simple fundamental law $F = ma$. Laws explain only when they can be expressed by simple principles or differential equations. It is often the case that the complicated patterns we see in spacetime can be derived from simple rules that we call laws.

Fundamental laws need not be time-directed or time-dependent. They may govern purely spatial distribution of matter. For example, Gauss's law

$$\nabla \cdot \mathbf{E} = \rho \tag{4}$$

in classical electrodynamics – one of Maxwell's equations – governs the distribution of electric charges and the electric field in space.

Often the explanation that laws provide involves deriving striking, novel, and unexpected patterns from simple laws. The relative contrast between the simplicity of the law and the complexity and richness of the patterns may indicate that the law is the correct explanation of the patterns.

For a toy example, consider the Mandelbrot set in the complex plane (Figure 6), produced by the simple rule that a complex number c is in the set just in case the function

---

[12] This type of explanation, sometimes called "constraint explanation," has been explored in the causation literature by Ben-Menahem (2018) and noncausal explanation literature by Lange (2016). Their accounts, with suitable modifications, may apply here. See Hildebrand (2013) for a critical discussion of primitive laws and explanations. His criticisms to primitivism are addressed by the introduction of Epistemic Guides on MinP.

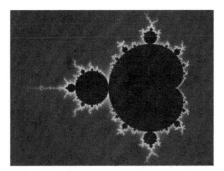

Figure 6 The Mandelbrot set with continuously colored environment. Picture created by Wolfgang Beyer with the program Ultra Fractal 3, CC BY-SA 3.0, https://creativecommons.org/licenses/by-sa/3.0, via Wikimedia Commons

$$f_c(z) = z^2 + c \tag{5}$$

does not diverge when iterated starting from $z = 0$. (For example, $c = -1$ is in this set but $c = 1$ is not, since the sequence $(0, -1, 0, -1, 0, -1, \ldots)$ is bounded but $(0, 1, 2, 5, 26, 677, 458330, \ldots)$ is not. For a nice description and visualization, see Penrose (1989, Ch. 4).) Here, a relatively simple rule yields a surprisingly intricate and rich pattern in the complex plane, a striking example of what is called the fractal structure. Now regard the Mandelbrot set as corresponding to the distribution of matter over (a two-dimensional) spacetime, the fundamental law for the world might be the rule just described. What is relevant here is that given just the pattern we may not expect it to be generated by any simple rule. It would be a profound discovery in that world to learn that its complicated structure is generated by the aforementioned rule based on the very simple function $f_c(z) = z^2 + c$. On our conception, it would be permissible to claim that the simple rule expresses the fundamental law, even though it is not a law for dynamic production. The Mandelbrot world is also an example of strong determinism, a theoretical possibility allowed on MinP.

The previous examples illustrate some features of explanation on MinP:

1. Laws explain by constraining the physical possibilities in an illuminating manner.
2. Nomic explanations (explanations given by laws) need not be dynamic explanations; indeed, they need not involve time at all.
3. Explanation by striking constraint can be especially illuminating when an intricate and rich pattern can be derived from a simple rule that expresses the constraint imposed by a law.

On MinP, more generally, there are two ingredients of a successful scientific explanation: a metaphysical element and an epistemic one. It must refer to the objective structure in the world, but it also must relate to our mind, remove puzzlement, and provide an understanding of nature. We suggest that a successful scientific explanation that fundamental laws provides should contain two aspects: (i) metaphysical fundamentality and (ii) simplicity.

The first aspect concerns the metaphysical status of fundamental laws: they should not be mere summaries of, or supervenient on, what actually happens; moreover, what the laws are should not depend on our actual practice or beliefs. This aspect is the *precondition* for having a non-Humean account of scientific explanations. On MinP, the precondition is fulfilled by postulating fundamental laws as primitive (metaphysically fundamental) facts that constrain the world. The constraint provides the needed *oomph* behind scientific explanations. Here lies the main difference between MinP and Humean Reductionism.

The second aspect concerns how fundamental laws relate to us. Constraints, in and of themselves, do not always provide satisfying explanations. Many constraints are complicated and thus insufficient for understanding nature. What we look for in the final theory of physics is not just any constraint but simple, compelling ones that ground observed complexities of an often bewildering variety. The explanation they provide corresponds to an insight or realization that leads us to say, "Aha! Now I understand." Often, simplicity is related to elegance or beauty. As Penrose reminds us:

> Elegance and simplicity are certainly things that go very much together. But nevertheless it cannot be quite the whole story. I think perhaps one should say it has to do with *unexpected* simplicity, where one imagines that things are going to be complicated but suddenly they turn out to be very much simpler than expected. It is not unnatural that this should be pleasing to the mind. (Penrose 1974, p.268)

The sense of unexpected simplicity is illustrated in the toy example of the Mandelbrot set as well as the laws discovered by Newton, Schrödinger, and Einstein.

Moreover, the second aspect of scientific explanation is connected to Epistemic Guides. It is obvious that fundamental laws should be empirically adequate and consistent with all phenomena. But why should we expect them to be simple? That is a challenging question that can be raised on any account of laws, including versions of Humeanism. We postpone the discussion to Section 5.

3.3 Examples and Further Clarifications

To further clarify MinP, I discuss some examples of dynamical laws and non-dynamical constraint laws. There is no difficulty accommodating them, as they can be understood as laws that constrain physical possibilities. Laws that involve intrinsic randomness present an interesting challenge.

3.3.1 Dynamical Laws

Let us take a dynamical law to be any law that determines how objects move or things change. Sometimes the label is restricted to dynamical laws that can be understood as FLOTEs that guide the development of the universe in time.

Hamilton's Equations. Consider classical mechanics for N particles, described by Hamilton's equations of motion (2) with a Hamiltonian specified in (3), a paradigmatic example of a FLOTE. Hamilton's equations are differential equations of a particular type: they admit initial value formulations. An intuitive way of thinking about dynamical laws is to understand them as evolving the initial state of the world into later ones. However, this view is not entirely natural for such a system. The view requires momenta to be part of the intrinsic state of the world at a time; but it seems more natural to regard them as aspects of extended trajectories, spanning continuous intervals of time. Regarding governing as dynamic production leads to awkward questions about instantaneous states and whether they include velocities and momenta.

The situation becomes even more complicated with relativistic spacetimes having no preferred foliation of equal-time hypersurfaces. If there is no objective fact about which events are simultaneous, there is no unique prior Cauchy surface that is responsible for the production of any later state. This seems to detract from the intuitive idea of dynamic production as a relation with an objective input, making it less natural in a relativistic setting.[13]

Instead of demanding that laws govern by producing subsequent states from earlier ones, we can regard laws as constraining the physical possibilities of spacetime and its contents. There is no difficulty accommodating Hamilton's equations or any other type of dynamical laws. A dynamical law specifies a set of histories of the system and need not be interpreted as presupposing a fundamental direction of time. The histories the laws allow can often be understood as direction-less histories, descriptions of which events are temporally between which other events.

A dynamical law such as (2) governs the actual world by constraining its history to be one allowed by (2). And MinP requires no privileged splitting of spacetime into space and time, as the physical possibilities can be stated in a completely coordinate-free way in terms of the contents of the four-dimensional spacetime.

---

[13] Christopher Dorst raised a similar point in personal communication. See also Dorst (2023).

Principles of Least Action. Besides dynamical laws of Hamiltonian form, other kinds of equations and principles are often employed even for Hamiltonian systems. Consider, for example, Hamilton's principle of least action: this requires that for a system of N particles with Cartesian coordinates $q = (q_1, q_2, \ldots, q_N)$:

$$\delta S = 0, \tag{6}$$

where $S = \int_{t_1}^{t_2} L(q(t), \dot{q}, t)dt$, with $\dot{q} = q(t)/dt$, δ the first-order variation of S corresponding to small variation in $q(t)$ with $q(t_1)$ and $q(t_2)$ fixed, and L, the Lagrangian, is the kinetic energy minus the potential energy of the system of N particles. While mathematically equivalent to Hamilton's equations, the principle of least action feels very different from a law expressing dynamic production. For those who take dynamic production to be constitutive of governing, the principle of least action cannot be the fundamental governing law. They would presumably need to insist that the universe is genuinely governed by some law of a form such as (2), with the principle of least action arising as a theorem. On MinP, there is no problem regarding the principle of least action as a candidate fundamental law, with no need for it to be derived from anything else. For a universe to obey the principle, its history must be one compatible with (6). That is the sense in which it would govern our universe.

Wheeler–Feynman Electrodynamics. Physicists have also considered dynamical equations that cannot be reformulated in Hamiltonian form. On MinP, there is no prohibition against laws expressed by such equations. For example, Wheeler and Feynman (1945, 1949) considered equations of motion for charged particles that involve both retarded fields (F_{ret}) and advanced ones (F_{adv}). On their theory, the trajectory of a charged particle depends on charge distributions in the past (corresponding to F_{ret}) as well as those in the future (corresponding to F_{adv}). Since the total field acting on particle j is $F_{tot} = \sum_{k \neq j} \frac{1}{2}({}^{(k)}F_{ret} + {}^{(k)}F_{adv})$, the equation of motion for particle j of mass m_j, charge e_j, and spacetime location q_j is

$$m_j \ddot{q}_j^{\mu} = e_j \sum_{k \neq j} \frac{1}{2} \left({}^{(k)}F_{ret}^{\mu\nu} + {}^{(k)}F_{adv}^{\mu\nu} \right) \dot{q}_{j,\nu} \tag{7}$$

with the dot the time derivative with respect to proper time, ${}^{(k)}F_{ret}$ the retarded field contributed by the past trajectory of particle k, and ${}^{(k)}F_{adv}$ the advanced one, involving the future trajectory of particle k. (For more details, see Deckert (2010) and Lazarovici (2018).) It is unclear how to understand equation (7) in terms of dynamic production. In contrast, it is clear on MinP: the fundamental law corresponding to such equations can be regarded as imposing a constraint on all trajectories of charged particles in spacetime.

Retrocausal Quantum Mechanics. There have been proposed reformulations of quantum mechanics that involve two independent wave functions of the universe: $\Psi_i(t)$ evolving from the past and $\Psi_f(t)$ evolving from the future. Some such proposals, motivated by a desire to evade no-go theorems or preserve time-symmetry, implement retrocausality or backward-in-time causal influences (Friederich and Evans 2019). Consider Sutherland (2008)'s causally symmetric Bohm model, which specifies an equation of motion governing N particles moving in a three-dimensional space under the influence of both $\Psi_i(t)$ and $\Psi_f(t)$:

$$\frac{d\boldsymbol{Q}_j(t)}{dt} = \frac{Re(\frac{\hbar}{2im_ja}\Psi_f^*\nabla_j\Psi_i)}{Re(\frac{1}{a}\Psi_f^*\Psi_i)}(Q(t),t) \tag{8}$$

with $Q(t) = (\boldsymbol{Q}_1(t),\ldots,\boldsymbol{Q}_N(t)) \in \mathbb{R}^{3N}$ the configuration of the N particles at time t, m_j the mass of particle j, and $a = \int \Psi_f^*(q,t)\Psi_i(q,t)dq$. It is unclear whether Sutherland's theory is viable; it also has many strange consequences. Nevertheless, MinP is compatible with regarding equation (8) as expressing a fundamental law that constrains particle trajectories in spacetime (even though we may have other reasons to not endorse the theory).

The Einstein Equation. In general relativity, the fundamental equation is the Einstein equation:

$$R_{\mu\nu} - \frac{1}{2}Rg_{\mu\nu} = k_0 T_{\mu\nu} + \Lambda g_{\mu\nu}, \tag{9}$$

where $R_{\mu\nu}$ is the Ricci tensor, R is the Ricci scalar, $g_{\mu\nu}$ is the metric tensor, $T_{\mu\nu}$ is the stress–energy tensor, Λ is the cosmological constant, $k_0 = 8\pi G/c^4$ with G Newton's gravitational constant and c the speed of light. Roughly speaking, the Einstein equation is a constraint on the relation between the geometry of spacetime and the distribution of matter (matter-energy) in spacetime. On MinP, we have no problem taking the equation itself as expressing a fundamental law of nature, one that constrains the actual spacetime and its contents. If Equation (9) governs our world in the sense of MinP, then (9) expresses a fundamental fact that does not supervene on or reduce to the actual spacetime and its contents.

There are ways of converting Equation (9) into FLOTEs that are suitable for a dynamic productive interpretation. If certain constraints are met, the Einstein equation can be decomposed in such a way that evolves an "initial data" of a three-dimensional hypersurface forward in time. A famous example is the ADM formalism (Arnowitt et al. 1962). However, they often discard certain solutions (such as spacetimes that are not globally hyperbolic). For non-Humeans who take dynamic production as constitutive for governing or explanations, those reformulations will be necessary. For them, the true laws of spacetime geometry should presumably be expressed by equations that describe the evolution of a three-geometry in time. In contrast, on MinP there is no metaphysical problem for taking the original Einstein equation as a fundamental law. The Einstein equation is simple and elegant and is generally regarded as the fundamental law in general relativity. We prefer not to discard or modify it on metaphysical grounds.

The Einstein equation allows some peculiar solutions. A particularly striking class of examples are spacetimes with closed timelike curves (CTCs). For MinP, there would seem to be no fundamental reason why such a possibility should be precluded. But the possibility of CTCs is precluded if we insist on dynamic production, since CTCs may lead to an event that dynamically produces itself.

3.3.2 Non-dynamical Constraint Laws

The examples mentioned earlier are explicitly related to trajectories spanning extended intervals of time. There are also important equations and principles that are not. We call them non-dynamical constraint laws. The minimal notion of governing easily applies to them. For example, some purely spatial constraints on the universe may be thought of as laws. In Section 3.2 we considered two examples of such laws – (4) and (5). Here we consider some more.

The Past Hypothesis. In the foundations of statistical mechanics and thermodynamics, followers of Boltzmann have proposed a candidate fundamental law of physics that Albert (2000) calls the Past Hypothesis (PH). It is a special boundary condition that is postulated to explain the emergent asymmetries of time in our universe, such as the Second Law of Thermodynamics. Here is one way to state it:

PH At one temporal boundary of the universe, the universe is in a low-entropy state.

This statement of PH is vague. We may be able to make it more precise by specifying the low-entropy state in terms of the thermodynamic properties of the universe or in terms of some geometrical properties (Penrose 1979). Penrose's version in general relativity, called the Weyl curvature hypothesis (WCH), renders it as follows:

WCH The Weyl curvature C_{abcd} vanishes at any "initial" singularity.

(For an extension of this idea to loop quantum cosmology, see Ashtekar and Gupt (2016a, b).) Let us use Ω_{PH} to denote the set of worlds compatible with

PH. If it is plausible that PH is a candidate fundamental law (Chen 2023a), then the metaphysical account of laws should make room for a boundary condition to be a fundamental law. On MinP, such an account is no problem. Together, PH and dynamical laws can govern the actual world by constraining it to be one among the histories compatible with all of them. They require the actual world (history) lie in the intersection $\Omega^{PH} \cap \Omega^{DL}$, where the second conjunct denotes the set of histories compatible with the dynamical laws. However, PH is not a governing law in the sense of dynamic production.

The Initial Projection Hypothesis. In a quantum universe, we have theoretical resources to postulate a stronger version of PH where the law selects a particular initial microstate, represented by a mixed-state density matrix. In Chen (2021a), I call this the Initial Projection Hypothesis (IPH):

IPH At one temporal boundary of the universe, the universal quantum state is the normalized projection onto the Past-Hypothesis subspace.

This version of the boundary-condition law can be exact without incurring a theoretical cost called untraceability (Chen 2022b). Since it pins down a unique initial microstate (in terms of a fundamental density matrix), together with the deterministic evolution equation for the quantum state, IPH yields a strongly deterministic theory.

The No-Boundary Proposal. A famous initial condition for a quantum universe, proposed by two pioneers of quantum cosmology Hartle and Hawking (1983), is the idea that the universe has no temporal boundaries; the spacetime geometry smoothly rounds off and shrinks to a point in the "past." They call it the No-Boundary Wave Function (NBWF):

NBWF The universal quantum state satisfies the Hartle-Hawking formula (1983), calculated over certain spacetime geometries that shrink to a point in the "past."

NBWF was proposed to solve the problem that quantum cosmology does not yield any prediction unless one posits a boundary condition. Hartle (1996, 1997) regards this as a fundamental law of the universe on par with the dynamic laws. If the Hartle–Hawking formula yields a unique solution of the wave function of the entire spacetime, the theory will also be strongly deterministic.

Conservation Laws and Symmetry Principles. According to a traditional perspective, symmetries such as those of rotation, spatial translation, and time translation are properties of the specific equations of motion. By Noether's theorem, those symmetries yield various conservation laws as theorems rather than postulates that need to be put in by hand. On that perspective, symmetries and conservation laws can be regarded as ontologically derivative of the fundamental laws, and are compatible with all metaphysical views on laws.

According to a more recent perspective, symmetries are fundamental. See for example: Wigner (1985, 1964) and Weinberg (1992). Lange (2009) calls them *metalaws*. For example, Wigner describes symmetries as "laws which the laws of nature have to obey" (Wigner 1985, p.700) and suggest that "there is a great similarity between the relation of the laws of nature to the events on one hand, and the relation of symmetry principles to the laws of nature on the other" (Wigner 1964, p.957). I do not take a firm stance on this perspective. Nevertheless, the perspective is compatible with MinP. If there is a symmetry principle K that a fundamental law of nature L must obey, then both K and L are fundamental facts, where K constrains L in the sense that the physical possibilities generated by L are invariant under the symmetry principle K, and any other possible fundamental laws are also constrained by K. This introduces further "modal" relations in the fundamental facts beyond just the constraining of the spacetime and its contents by L.

Methodologically, one might prefer theories with dynamical laws, especially FLOTEs, to those without them. MinP allows this preference. Even though MinP does not restrict laws to FLOTEs, the principle of Epistemic Guides suggests that we look for simple and informative laws. FLOTEs, when they admit initial value formulations, may come with such theoretical virtues (Callender 2017, Chs. 7–8). The preference for FLOTEs and dynamical laws more generally may be explained by a preference for laws that strike a good balance between simplicity and informativeness.

3.3.3 Probabilistic Laws

Candidate fundamental physical theories can also employ probability measures and distributions. Such measures and distributions can be objective, and they may be called objective probabilities. The probabilistic postulates in physical theories can be lawlike, even though the nature of those probabilities is a controversial issue.

There are two types of probabilistic postulates in physics: (i) stochastic dynamics and (ii) probabilistic boundary conditions. We start with (i) as it is more familiar. Consider the Ghirardi–Rimini–Weber theory in quantum mechanics, a theory in which observers and measurements do not have a central place and in which the quantum wave function spontaneously collapses according to precise probabilistic rules. On the GRW theory, the wave function of the universe $\Psi(t)$ evolves unitarily according to the Schrödinger equation but is interrupted by random collapses. The probabilities of where and when the collapses occur are fixed by the theory. (For details, see Ghirardi et al. (1986) and Ghirardi (2018).)

For an example of (ii), consider Albert and Loewer's Mentaculus theory of statistical mechanics, where they postulate, in addition to PH and the dynamical equations (such as (2) and (3)), a probabilistic distribution of the initial microstate of the universe:

Statistical Postulate (SP) At the temporal boundary of the universe when PH applies, the probability distribution of the microstate of the universe is given by the uniform one (according to the natural measure) that is supported on the macrostate of the universe (compatible with PH).

One may also understand it in terms of typicality: that we regard the initial probability distribution to pick out a measure of almost all or the overwhelming majority – a measure of typicality (Goldstein 2001, 2012). On this way of thinking, SP says the following:

SP' At the temporal boundary of the universe when PH applies, the initial microstate of the universe is typical inside the macrostate of the universe (according to the natural measure of typicality).

On the basis of SP', one can then explore what the theory says about typical histories and apply it to our universe.

A similar probabilistic boundary condition appears in Bohmian mechanics, where one can interpret the initial probability distribution of particle configuration as representing a typicality measure:

$$\rho_{t_0}(q) = |\Psi(q, t_0)|^2, \tag{10}$$

where t_0 is when PH applies and $\Psi(q, t_0)$ is the wave function of the universe at t_0. Based on this measure, almost all worlds governed by Bohmian mechanics will exhibit the Born rule. (For more details, see Dürr et al. (1992) and Goldstein (2017).)

In fact, it is also possible to interpret stochastic dynamics as yielding a typicality measure: the GRW theory specifies a probability distribution over entire histories of the quantum states, and what matters is the behavior of "almost all" of those possible histories.

Probability measures and typicality measures are not straightforwardly understandable in terms of MinP: it is not clear how they should be understood in terms of constraints. The difficulty is greater for stochastic dynamics.

On the typicality approach, one has the option to regard the measures picked out by the probabilistic boundary conditions as referring to something methodological instead of nomological – how in practice one decides whether a law is supported or refuted by evidence. However, the probabilities in the stochastic dynamics are clearly nomological and not just a methodological principle of theory choice.

Chen and Goldstein (2022, sect. 3.3.3) discuss five interpretive strategies that are available on MinP. Barrett and Chen (2023) have recently proposed a constraint account of probabilistic laws, where the nomic constraint is expressed in terms of Martin-Löf randomness. The proposal is attractive from the perspective of MinP, since it provides a unified basis for understanding all candidate laws in terms of constraining laws. However, there is much room for future work. As I shall discuss later, the problem of probabilistic laws is difficult on all accounts of laws. Solving it may turn on questions about the relation between probability and typicality, and their relation to physical possibility.

3.4 Summary

MinP is an intelligible and attractive proposal for understanding fundamental laws of nature. It vindicates the non-Humean conviction that laws govern while remaining flexible enough to accommodate the variety of kinds of laws entertained in physics. In particular, it does not require that laws presume a fundamental direction of time. MinP illuminates metaphysics but is not unduly constrained by it.

4 Other Accounts

In this section, I survey five influential accounts of laws and compare them to MinP: Humean Reductionism, Platonic Reductionism, Aristotelian Reductionism, Langean Reductionism, and Maudlinian Primitivism. With the exception of Humean Reductionism, they are more restrictive than MinP because of their metaphysical posits. Moreover, two of them–Aristotelian Reductionism and Maudlinian Primitivism–are explicitly committed to a fundamental direction of time.

4.1 Humean Reductionism

We start with Humean Reductionism, a metaphysically austere account that is as flexible as MinP (if not more so). On this view, laws do not govern but merely summarize what actually happens in the world. Fundamental reality consists solely in the *Humean mosaic*, a concrete example of which is a four-dimensional spacetime occupied by particles and fields. At the fundamental level, laws of nature do not exist and do not move stuff around. Laws are derivative of and ontologically dependent on the actual Humean mosaic. The laws are the way they are *because of* what the actual trajectories of particles and histories of fields are, not the other way around, in contrast to the governing picture of laws, such as the one given by MinP. On MinP, the patterns in the Humean mosaic are ultimately explained by the laws; on Humean Reductionism, the laws are ultimately explained by the Humean mosaic, which in turn is not really explained by anything.

Following Ramsey, Lewis (1973, 1983, 1986) proposes a "best-system" analysis of laws that shows how laws can be recovered from the Humean mosaic. The basic idea is that laws are certain regularities of the Humean mosaic. However, not any regularity is a law, since some are accidental. One needs to be selective about which regularities to count as laws. Lewis suggests we pick those regularities in the best system of true sentences about the Humean mosaic. The strategy is to consider various systems (collections) of true sentences about the Humean mosaic and pick the system that strikes the best balance among various theoretical virtues, such as simplicity and informativeness.

For a concrete example, let the Humean mosaic (the fundamental ontology) be a Minkowski spacetime occupied by massive, charged particles and an electromagnetic field. The locations and properties of those particles and the strengths and directions of the field at different points in spacetime is the matter distribution, which corresponds to the local matters of particular fact. Suppose the matter distribution is a solution to Maxwell's equations. Consider three systems of true statements (characterized below using the axioms of the systems) about this mosaic:

- System 1: {Spacetime point (x_1, y_1, z_1, t_1) has field strengths E_1 and B_1 with directions $\vec{v}_1$ and $\vec{v}_{1'}$ and is occupied by a particle of charge q_1; spacetime point (x_2, y_2, z_2, t_2) has field strengths E_2 and B_2 with directions $\vec{v}_2$ and $\vec{v}_{2'}$ and is not occupied by a charged particle; ......}
- System 2: {"Things exist."}
- System 3: {Maxwell's equations, the Lorentz force equation, and Newton's law of motion}

System 1 lists all the facts about spacetime points one by one. It has much informational content but it is complicated. System 2 is just one sentence that says there are things but does not tell us what they are and how they are distributed. It is extremely simple but has little informational content. System 3 contains six equations. It has less information about the world than System 1 but has much more than System 2. It is more complicated than System 2 but much less so than System 1. System 1 and System 2 are two extremes; they have one virtue too much at the complete expense of the other. In contrast, System 3 strikes a good balance between simplicity and informativeness. System 3 is the best system of the mosaic. Therefore, according to the best-system analysis, the axioms of System 3 are the fundamental laws of this world.

On this approach and unlike on MinP, laws are not fundamental facts that govern the universe, but are merely descriptive of and derivative from the Humean mosaic. Laws do not push or pull things, enforce behaviors, or produce the patterns. Laws are just winners in a competition among systematic summaries of the mosaic. Beebee (2000) calls it the "non-governing conception of laws of nature." Laws are merely those generalizations which figure in the most economical true axiomatization of all the particular matters of fact that happen to obtain.

Despite the simplicity and appeal of Lewis's analysis, there is an obstacle. The theoretical virtue of simplicity is language-dependent. For example, suppose there is a predicate F that applies to all and only things in the actual spacetime. Consider the following system:

- System 4: $\{\forall x F(x)\}$

This is informationally equivalent to System 1 and more informative than System 3, and yet it is simpler than System 3. If we allow competing systems to use predicate F, there will be a system (namely System 4) that is overall better than System 3. Given the best-system analysis, the actual laws of the mosaic would not be Maxwell's equations but "$\forall x F(x)$." To rule out such degenerate systems, Lewis places a restriction on language. Suitable systems that enter into the competition can invoke predicates that refer to only natural properties. For example, the predicate "having negative charge" refers to a natural property, while the disjunctive predicate "having negative charge or being the Eiffel Tower" refers to a less natural property. Some properties are perfectly natural, such as those invoked in fundamental physics about mass, charge, spacetime location, and so on. It is those perfectly natural properties that the axioms in the best system must refer to. The predicate F applies to all and only things in the actual world, which makes up an "unnatural" set of entities. F is not perfectly natural; it is an example of a *gruesome* predicate connected to Goodman's problem of induction (Section 2.6). Hence, System 4 is not suitable. The requirement that the axioms of the best system refers only to perfectly natural properties is an important element of Lewis's Humeanism.

Over the years, Lewis and his followers have, in various ways, extended and modified the best-system analysis of laws on Humean Reductionism. I have elsewhere called the updated view *Reformed Humeanism about Laws*, but for simplicity here I will just call it the Best System Account (BSA):

Best System Account (BSA) The fundamental laws are the axioms of the best system that summarizes the mosaic and optimally balances simplicity, informativeness, fit, and degree of naturalness of the properties referred to. The mosaic contains only local matters of particular facts, and the mosaic is the complete collection of fundamental facts.

BSA can accommodate various kinds of laws of nature. Without going into too much detail, we note the following features:

1. Chance. Although chance is not an element of the Humean mosaic, it can appear in the best system. Humeans can introduce probability distributions as axioms of the best system (Lewis 1980). This works nicely for stochastic theories such as the GRW theory. Humeans can evaluate the contribution of the probability distributions by using a new theoretical virtue called *fit*. A system is more fit than another just in case it assigns a higher (comparative) probability than the other does the history of the universe. For certain mosaics, the inclusion of probability in the best system can greatly improve the informational content without sacrificing too much simplicity. Hence, fit can be seen as the probabilistic extension of informativeness. Humeans can also allow what is called "deterministic chance" (Loewer 2001). Take a deterministic Newtonian theory of particle motion and add to it PH and SP, which can be represented as a uniform probabilistic distribution, conditionalized on a low-entropy macrostate of the universe at t_0. The Humean account of chance (both stochastic and deterministic) is arguably one of the simplest and clearest to date, but it still faces the Big Bad Bug (Lewis 1994) and the zero-fit problem (Elga 2004).

2. Flexibility with respect to the forms of laws. Humean Reductionism is entirely flexible regarding the forms of laws. Every example discussed in Section 3.3 can be regarded as a best-system law that figures in the optimal summary of the Humean mosaic. Lewis (1983) maintains that "only the regularities of the system are to count as laws" (p.367). However, there is no reason to limit the Humean account to laws about general facts (Callender 2004). This flexibility is a significant advantage Humean Reductionism has over some other accounts of laws (Loewer 2012).

3. Flexibility with respect to perfect naturalness. For Lewis, perfect naturalness is a property of properties. Perfectly natural properties pick out the same set of things as Armstrong's theory of sparse universals (more on that in Section 2.2). However, the chief motivation for Lewis's use of perfect naturalness is to rule out systems that use "gruesome" predicates. If that is the issue, as

Hicks and Schaer (2017) suggest, we can simply require that "degree of naturalness" of the predicates involved be a factor in the overall ranking of competing systems, and the best system should also optimally balance degree of naturalness of the predicates together with the rest of the theoretical virtues, such as simplicity, informativeness, and fit. The flexibility with respect to perfect naturalness also allows the best system to refer to nonfundamental properties such as entropy, as may be necessary if the Past Hypothesis is a fundamental law.

Comparisons with MinP. Humean Reductionism and MinP are similar in several respects. First, neither requires a fundamental direction of time, and both permit a reductionist understanding of it. Second, both views are flexible enough to accommodate the distinct kinds of laws entertained in physics.[14] Third, both views emphasize the importance of simplicity (and other theoretical virtues) in laws and scientific explanations.

Let me turn to their differences. First, on Humean Reductionism, the patterns in the Humean mosaic have no ultimate explanation; after all, the mosaic grounds what the laws are. Many reject Humean Reductionism for that reason.[15] On MinP, suitable explanations of the patterns must not be merely summaries of the mosaic. On MinP, fundamental laws are metaphysically fundamental facts that exist in addition to the mosaic. They govern the mosaic and explain its patterns by constraining it in an illuminating manner.

Second, they also differ regarding the modal profile of laws. This has been much discussed in the literature (see e.g. Carroll (1994) and Maudlin (2007)). On MinP, since fundamental laws are primitive facts, there can be a physically possible world corresponding to an empty Minkowski spacetime governed by the Einstein equation. However, on Humean Reductionism, that world is one where the simplest summary is just the laws of special relativity, and it is impossible to have such a world where the law is the Einstein equation (Maudlin 2007, pp. 67–68). To allow two worlds with the same mosaic (empty Minkowski spacetime) but different laws (laws of special relativity and those of general relativity), which is accepted in scientific practice, is to endorse nonsupervenience of the laws on the mosaic. Therefore, Humean Reductionism seems to be in conflict with scientific practice while MinP is not.[16]

---

[14] Humean reductionism of chancy or probabilistic laws is one of its selling points, as such laws are difficult to understand on non-Humeanism. However, Humean reductionism also faces its own problems with chance, such as the Big Bad Bug and the zero-fit problem mentioned earlier.

[15] There is an ongoing debate about the status and nature of explanation on Humeanism. For some examples, see Loewer (2012), Lange (2013), and Emery (2019, 2023). For a discussion that non-Humeanism offers better explanation than Humeanism, see Hildebrand (2022, Sect. 7).

[16] See Roberts (2008) for a Humean account of laws based on a contextualist semantics that may alleviate this worry.

Third, some Humeans suggest that, precisely because of the metaphysical difference concerning supervenience, Humeanism has an *epistemological advantage* over non-Humean views such as MinP (Earman and Roberts 2005). Since Humean laws are supervenient on the mosaic, and since the mosaic is all that we can empirically access (we do not directly see the laws), we are in a better position to determine laws on Humeanism than on non-Humeanism. This argument becomes less convincing once we remind ourselves that *we are not given the mosaic*; the mosaic in modern physics is as theoretical as the laws. I return to this point in Section 5.

Finally, Humean Reductionism faces what Lewis (1994) calls the problem of "ratbag idealism." Since the best systematization is constitutive of lawhood, and if what counts as best depends on us, lawhood may become mind-dependent. In contrast, on MinP, fundamental laws are what they are irrespective of our psychology and judgments of simplicity and informativeness. Hence, MinP respects our conviction about the objectivity and mind-independence of fundamental laws. See Section 7 for more discussions.

4.2 Platonic Reductionism

With Humean Reductionism, nothing ultimately explains the patterns in the Humean mosaic. Those with a governing conception of laws may seek to find a deeper explanation. In virtue of what is every massive particle in the world behaving according to the formula $F = ma$? What, if anything, enforces the pattern and makes sure nothing deviates from it? On MinP, it is the laws themselves.

Dretske (1977), Tooley (1977), and Armstrong (1983) propose a different non-Humean account of governing laws, one that seeks to understand them in terms of *universals*. The universals that they accept are in addition to things in the Humean mosaic. They are "over and above" the Humean mosaic. In traditional metaphysics, universals are repeatable entities that explain the genuine similarity of objects. Let us start with some mundane examples. Two cups are genuinely similar in virtue of their sharing a universal *Being a Cup*. The universal is something they both instantiate and something that explains their genuine similarity. A cup is different from a horse because the latter instantiates a different universal *Being a Horse*. Now, those universals are not fundamental, and they may be built from more fundamental universals about physical properties. Dretske, Tooley, and Armstrong use universals to provide explanations in science. For them, the paradigm examples are universals that correspond to fundamental physical properties, such as mass and charge. On their view, laws of nature hold because of a certain relation obtaining among such universals.

This theory of laws has connection to Plato's theory of forms.[17] Let us call it *Platonic Reductionism*.[18]

Consider the world where $F = ma$ holds for every massive particle. In such a world, any particle with mass m instantiates the universal *having mass m*, any particle under total force F instantiates the universal *being under total force F*, and any particle with acceleration F/m instantiates the universal *having acceleration F/m*. The universals are multiply instantiated and repeated, as there are many particles that share the same universals. Those universals give unity to the particles that instantiate them. The theory also postulates, as a fundamental fact, that the universal *having mass m* and the universal *being under total force F* necessitate the universal *having acceleration F/m*. Hence, if any particle instantiates *having mass m* and *being under total force F*, then it has to instantiate *having acceleration F/m*. It follows that every particle has to obey $F = ma$.[19] This adds the necessity and the oomph that are missing in Humean Reductionism.

With Platonic Reductionism, the regularity is explained by the metaphysical postulate of universals and the necessitation relation N that hold among universals. Following Hildebrand (2013), we may summarize it as follows:

Necessitation For all universals F and G, $N(F, G)$ necessitates the regularity that all Fs are Gs.

Some clarificatory remarks:

1. Universals. (i) The appeal to universals is indispensable in this theory of laws. The theory is committed to a fundamental ontology of objects (particulars) and a fundamental ontology of universals. Hence, Platonic Reductionism is incompatible with nominalism about universals. (ii) Defenders such as Armstrong appeal to a sparse theory of universals, where the fundamental universals correspond to the fundamental properties we find in fundamental physics. The sparse universals correspond to the perfectly natural properties that Lewis invokes in his account. Consider Lewis's example of the predicate F that denotes the property shared by all and only things in the actual world. For Armstrong, "$\forall x F(x)$" does not express a fundamental law because objects with property F are not genuinely similar, and F is a property that does not correspond to one of the fundamental, sparse universals.

---

[17] For an overview of Plato's theory of forms, see Kraut (2017).

[18] In the literature it is sometimes called the Dretske–Tooley–Armstrong (DTA) account of laws or the Universalist account of laws. Calling it Platonic *reductionism* may be controversial. But see the discussion in Carroll (1994, appendix A1).

[19] This example about $F = ma$ does not exactly fit in Armstrong's schema of "All F's are G." See Armstrong (1983, ch.7) for a proposal for accommodating "functional laws."

2. Necessity. (i) The necessity relation among universals is put into the theory by hand. It is a postulate that such a relation holds among universals and does necessitate regularities. (It is also postulated that the N relation among universals is itself a universal.) To some commentators, it is unclear why the postulate is justified (Lewis 1983, p.366). In response, a defender of Platonic Reductionism may take the necessity relation simply as a primitive and stipulate its connections to regularities (Schaffer 2016). This defense is also available on other non-Humean accounts.

(ii) Armstrong (1983, p.172) understands probabilistic laws as giving "a probability of necessitation" between two universals. What is "a probability of a necessitation?" Conceptually, whether F necessitates G seems like a matter that does not admit of degree. What does this probability mean, and how does it relate to actual frequencies and why should it constrain our credences? Even if one accepts the intelligibility of the necessitation relation, one may be unwilling to accept the intelligibility of objective probability of a necessitation and one may be puzzled by how the probability of a necessitation can explain the regularities.

On Platonic Reductionism, it is unclear how we should think about the direction of time. Even though there is a strong connection between the necessitation relation N and causation, it does not seem that the main defenders build the direction of time into N. Nevertheless, if Platonic Reductionism does not have room for treating the Past Hypothesis as a fundamental law, it may need to invoke a fundamental direction of time for worlds like ours. Perhaps Platonic Reductionism is best paired with a primitivism about the direction of time.

Comparisons with MinP. Platonic Reductionism and MinP agree that there are governing laws that do not supervene on the Humean mosaic, but disagree on whether governing laws should be analyzed in terms of or are reducible to relations among universals.

While Platonic Reductionism is ontologically committed to fundamental universals, MinP is not. I do not think that universals offer additional explanatory benefits. The motivating idea of Platonic Reductionism is that universals are properties that genuinely similar objects share, and it is partly in virtue of the universals shared by those objects that the objects behave in the same way everywhere and everywhen. The metaphysics of N is a complicated business, and it seems to create more mystery than it dispels. In contrast, on MinP there are fundamental laws that govern the world by constraining the physical possibilities. Explanation in terms of simple laws seems clear enough to vindicate the non-Humean intuition that there is something more than the mosaic that governs it. Moreover, MinP is compatible with various metaphysical views about properties such as realism and nominalism. A realist attitude toward laws does not require a realist attitudes toward properties.

Unlike MinP, Platonic Reductionism places restrictions on the form of fundamental laws. On Platonic Reductionism, all laws need to be recast in the form of relations among universals, and it is unclear how to do so for laws in modern physics (see also Hildebrand and Metcalf (2021, Sect 3.2).) Consider a differential equation that expresses a candidate fundamental law such as (2). What are the universals that they actually relate? Assuming that velocity and acceleration are derived quantities, what are the universals that correspond to the derivatives on either side of the equations? Armstrong argues that universals must be instantiated in some concrete particulars. As Wilson observes (p.439), differential equations conflict with Armstrong's principle about the instantiation of universals, as the values of the derivatives are calculated from values possessed by non-actual states (those in the small neighborhood around the actual one) that are not instantiated. In contrast, MinP has no difficulty accommodating laws expressed by differential equations.

Moreover, some candidate fundamental laws involve properties that do not seem to correspond to universals. For example, PH applies to only one moment in time. As such, it is a spatiotemporally restricted law that seems in tension with the approach involving universals (universal, repeatable, and multiply instantiated). Tooley (1977) considers an example of Smith's Garden, and there he seems open to accept spatiotemporally restricted laws if they are significant enough. One can devise semantic tricks to understand them in terms of universals, but it is hard to see what the point is. In contrast, MinP has no difficulty accommodating spatiotemporally restricted laws; they can function perfectly as constraints on the universe that are about specific places or times.

4.3 Aristotelian Reductionism

The next view is most commonly associated with contemporary defenders of dispositional essentialism. On this view, laws are not fundamental entities; neither do they govern the world in any metaphysically robust sense. Laws do not push or pull things around. Instead, the patterns we see are explained by the fundamental properties that objects instantiate. Those properties are the seats of metaphysical powers, necessity, and oomph. Those properties make objects, in a certain sense, "active" (Ellis 2001, p.1). Such properties are often called "dispositions," and also sometimes called "powers," "capacities," "potentialities," and "potencies."[20] However, they are different from the universals in Platonic

---

[20] For an overview of the metaphysics of dispositions, see Choi and Fara (2021).

Reductionism or the natural properties in Humean Reductionism, which may be viewed as "passive." If there are any laws (and there is an internal debate about this question among defenders of this fundamental dispositional ontology), they derive from or originate in the fundamental dispositions of material objects.

Roughly speaking, objects with dispositions have characteristic behaviors (also called manifestation) in response to certain stimuli (Bird 2007, p.3). For example, a glass has a disposition to shatter when struck; an ice cube has a disposition to melt when heated; salt has a disposition to dissolve when put into water. On this view, fundamental properties are similarly dispositional: negatively charged particles have a disposition to attract positively charged particles; massive particles have a disposition to accelerate in a way that is proportional to the total forces on them and inversely proportional to their masses. Moreover, a dispositional essentialist holds that some properties have dispositional essences, which means that their essences can be characterized in dispositional terms.[21]

Among those who endorse a dispositionalist fundamental ontology, not everyone accepts that fundamental laws, which are usually taken to be universally valid and always true, arise from dispositions. For example, Cartwright (1983, 1994) and Mumford (2004) deny the need for such laws. Nevertheless, the dispositional essentialists need not abandon laws. They can maintain that laws supervene on or reduce to dispositions. Because of its Aristotelian roots (Ellis 2014), we call such a view *Aristotelian Reductionism* about laws.[22] Aristotelian Reductionists maintain that (i) the metaphysical powers, necessity, and oomph reside in the fundamental dispositions; (ii) laws are metaphysically derivative of the dispositions; (iii) laws are metaphysically necessary.

How are laws derived from dispositions? Bird proposes that we can derive laws from certain counterfactual conditionals associated with dispositional essences. A more recent approach is that of Demarest (2017, 2021) and Kimpton-Nye (2017) that seek to combine a dispositional fundamental ontology with a best-system analysis of lawhood. Let us focus on the approach of Demarest. She proposes that dispositions (she follows Bird and calls them potencies) do metaphysical work. They produce their characteristic behaviors, resulting in patterns in nature. Their characteristic behaviors, in different possible worlds, can be summarized in simple and informative axiomatic systems,

---

[21] Some, such as Bird (2007), go further and claim that all perfectly natural properties in Lewis (1986)'s sense or all sparse universals in Armstrong (1983)'s sense have dispositional essences.

[22] Many defenders of this view suggest that even though it has roots in Aristotle, it is not committed to many aspects of Aristotelianism.

and the best one contains the true laws of nature. That is like Humean Reductionism except that (i) Demarest's fundamental ontology includes potencies and (ii) the summary is not of just the actual distribution of potencies but also all merely possible ones. In this way, her proposal may be an alternative development of Bird's suggestion that we can derive laws from potencies, though she does not rely on counterfactuals.

In contrast to Humean Reductionism, here the patterns are ultimately explained by the potencies. How do potencies explain? Demarest appeals to dynamic production (Demarest 2017, pp.51–52). The potencies at an earlier time explain how things move at a later time by dynamically producing, determining, or generating the patterns. Demarest's view seems committed to a fundamental direction of time. The account of dynamic explanation presupposes a fundamental distinction between past and future, that is between the initial and the subsequent states of the world. The initial arrangement of particles and potencies metaphysically ground subsequent behaviors of particles. The commitment of a fundamental direction of time does not seem optional on her view.

Moreover, the metaphysical framework of fundamental dispositions already seems committed to a fundamental direction of time, independently of the issue of laws. For example, it is natural to interpret the discussions by Ellis, Bird, Mumford as suggesting that the manifestation of a disposition cannot be temporally prior to its stimulus, which presupposes a fundamental direction of time.[23] Therefore, although Aristotelian Reductionism does away with the governing conception of laws, the view seems committed to a fundamental direction of time twice over.

Comparisons with MinP. Aristotelian Reductionists do not think that laws govern in a metaphysically robust sense. In contrast, MinP vindicates the conviction that laws do. Aristotelian Reductionism is committed to a fundamental ontology of dispositions. MinP is not. Most physicists today may be unfamiliar with the concept of fundamental dispositions. They are familiar with the concept of fundamental laws and how they figure in various scientific explanations. Hence, MinP seems more science-friendly.

Moreover, it is natural to read dispositional essentialists such as Bird, Mumford, and Ellis as having an implicit commitment to a fundamental direction of time. Demarest's account is more explicit in linking the dispositional essentialist ontology and the account of nomic explanations to that of dynamic metaphysical dependence, or what I call dynamic production. As noted in

---

[23] In contrast, Vetter (2015) is open to a temporally symmetric metaphysics but assumes temporal asymmetry in her account of dispositions (which she calls potentialities).

Section 3.3, it is difficult to understand how dynamic production works even in simple cases such as Hamilton's equations and much less in relativistic spacetimes. Requiring dynamic production presumably rules out theories that permit CTCs, as well as purely spatial laws, or even worlds for which spacetime is emergent. In contrast, MinP is not committed to a fundamental direction of time, and MinP is entirely open to those possibilities (even though we may have other considerations, beyond the conception of laws, to not consider them).

Finally, there are problems specific to accounts (such as Bird's) that analyze laws in terms of dispositions. Bird (2007) lists four problems (p.211): (i) fundamental constants, (ii) conservation laws and symmetry principles, (iii) principles of least action, and (iv) multiple laws relating distinct properties. Problem (i) arises because slight differences in the constants do not require the properties to be different; problem (ii) because conservation laws and symmetry principles do not seem to be manifestations of dispositions; problem (iii) because the principles seem to commit to the physical possibilities of alternate histories, something not allowed on dispositional essentialism; problem (iv) because a third law relating two properties will not be the outcome of the dispositional natures of those properties. Such problems do not arise on MinP.

4.4 Langean Reductionism

Lange (1999, 2005, 2009) develops a non-Humean account where laws are explained by counterfactuals. He suggests that counterfactuals (instead of laws as on MinP) should be regarded as ontologically basic. Let us call the view *Langean Reductionism*. It is also more restrictive than MinP.

To unpack his views, we need to understand his definition of lawhood. Let us denote the set of (first-order) laws of nature together with their logical consequences as Λ. It is understood to include only what Lange (2009, p.17) calls "sub-nomic truths," those that do not directly make claims about lawhood, such as $F = ma$, but not *it is a law that $F = ma$*. On Lange's account (p.42), Λ stands in a special relationship to counterfactuals. He proposes that Λ is the "largest nonmaximal sub-nomically stable set" of truths about the universe. Roughly speaking, Λ is the largest set that is (1) not the set of all (sub-nomic) truths about the universe, and (2) counterfactually stable under any (sub-nomic) supposition that is consistent with Λ. To satisfy (2), Λ must be such that, for any sub-nomic proposition p that does not make claims about lawhood or conflict with Λ, every member of Λ would still be true if p were true.[24]

---

[24] For a more precise and complete definition of (2), which involves nested counterfactuals, see Lange (2009, p.29).

This special relationship between Λ and counterfactuals, on Lange's view, provides a principled and sharp distinction between laws and accidents. It allows us to define laws from counterfactuals in a noncircular way, achieving one of the central aims of Lange's project and distinguishing it from all other accounts in the literature.

The nonmaximality condition (1) plays a crucial role here. Lange shows that every set containing accidents, with the possible exception of the set of all sub-nomic truths, lacks the special property of sub-nomic stability. As Lange explains (p.30), on many logics of counterfactuals, the set of all sub-nomic truths (including all accidents) also forms a sub-nomically stable set, albeit a *maximal* one (because it cannot be expanded without becoming inconsistent). Without the further constraint that laws cannot form a maximal set, there will be no principled and sharp distinction between laws and accidents, for sub-nomic stability does not guarantee lawhood. One can define laws to be the stable set that contains no accidents, but that would be circular, a feature he wants to avoid. What does the trick is defining laws to be the largest *nonmaximal* sub-nomically stable set.

What make a proposition a law of nature are the associated counterfactuals, which are regarded by Lange as metaphysically fundamental. This reverses the direction of metaphysical explanation, as we usually think that laws support counterfactuals and not the other way around (Section 2.3). However, Lange does not deny that sometimes our knowledge of laws can be used to evaluate counterfactuals, even though laws depend on counterfactuals.

This view is arguably compatible with the Past Hypothesis being a fundamental law. Hence, it is compatible with a reductionist understanding of the direction of time, and it does not assume that laws must dynamically produce the states of the universe in order to govern.

Comparisons with MinP. Langean reductionism is one of the more flexible non-Humean accounts of laws, as it can accommodate a wide variety of laws. However, it is still more restrictive than MinP. Because Lange requires that Λ be nonmaximal, Langean Reductionism is incompatible with even the metaphysical possibility of strong determinism.

To see the conflict, let us suppose strong determinism is metaphysically possible. Consider a possible world w where strong determinism is true. The laws of w is compatible with only w. Thus, the Λ at w, being logically closed, entails all (sub-nomic) truths at w. That makes Λ the *maximal* sub-nomically stable set at w, contradicting the requirement that Λ be nonmaximal. Hence, defining Λ to be nonmaximal rules out the *metaphysical possibility* of strong determinism.

I regard that as a significant and under-appreciated cost of Lange's account. Strong determinism is logically consistent and conceptually coherent. On what grounds are we entitled to dismiss it as metaphysically impossible? Moreover, there can be scientifically motivated, empirically adequate, and theoretically virtuous candidates for laws that are strongly deterministic and provide new insights into the foundations of physics (Sections 2.4 and 3.3). Ruling out strong determinism by fiat seems contrary to the methodology of naturalistic metaphysics. I think the lesson here is that we should rethink the original motivation for a noncircular distinction between laws and accidents and modify Lange's account in light of the possibility of strong determinism.

In contrast, strong determinism is not only allowed on MinP but serves as a good example of how laws constrain the universe – strongly deterministic laws rules out every world except the actual world. If such laws are simple, they provide strong and compelling explanation for every fundamental event in spacetime.

4.5 Maudlinian Primitivism

All previous accounts surveyed in this section attempt to reduce laws to something else, such as the Humean mosaic, universals, dispositions, and counterfactuals. An alternative view is simply to take laws as ontological primitives. An influential primitivist account is developed by Maudlin (2007). His version of primitivism, which in one aspect is similar to MinP, comes with more metaphysical commitments than MinP.

As a primitivist about laws, he suggests that we should not analyze or reduce laws into anything else. Maudlin is also committed to primitivism about the direction of time: that the distinction between past and future is metaphysically fundamental and not reducible to anything else. Maudlin combines the two commitments into a metaphysical package (p.182).

For Maudlin, laws produce or generate later states of the world from earlier ones. In this way, via the productive power of the laws, subsequent states of the world (and its parts) are explained by earlier ones and ultimately by the initial state of the universe. This idea about productive explanation, for example, allows Maudlin's account to vindicate a widespread intuition about Bromberger's flagpole. The shadow is produced by the circumstances and the length of the pole (together with the laws). Although we can deduce from the laws the pole length based on the circumstances and the shadow length, the pole length is not produced by them. Hence, given the laws, the pole length and the circumstances explain, but are not explained by, the shadow length.

Maudlin suggests that his package yields an attractive picture by being closer to our initial conception of the world. He is committed to all three theses discussed in Section 2.4: Only FLOTEs, Dynamic Production, and Temporal Direction Primitivism. We may summarize the package as follows:

Maudlinian Primitivism Fundamental laws are certain ontological primitives in the world. Only dynamical laws (in particular, laws of temporal evolution) can be fundamental laws. They operate on the universe by producing later states of the universe from earlier ones, in accord with the fundamental direction of time.

Maudlin allows there to be primitive stochastic dynamical laws—those laws that involve objective probability such as the GRW collapse laws. Hence, dynamic production need not be deterministic. An initial state can be compatible with multiple later states, determining only an objective probability distribution over those states. Perhaps the objective probability can be understood as *propensity*, with stochastic production implying variable propensities of producing various states, in proportion to their objective probabilities and in accord with the direction of time. However, even if deterministic production is an intelligible notion, it is not clear that stochastic production or propensity is as intelligible. (Compare this with the earlier point about "probabilistic necessitation" in Platonic Reductionism.)

Comparisons with MinP. Maudlinian Primitivism and MinP agree that fundamental laws are metaphysically fundamental and that they govern. They disagree about how they do it.

For Maudlin, dynamic production is essential, and every fundamental law needs to have the form of a dynamical law (in the narrow sense of a FLOTE). For laws to produce, they operate according to the fundamental direction of time, providing an intuitive picture close to our pre-theoretic conception of the world: "the universe is generated from a beginning and guided toward its future by physical law" (p.182). MinP is not committed to a fundamental direction of time; nor is it committed to dynamic production as how laws govern or explain. On MinP, explanation by simple constraint is good enough. Many candidate fundamental laws such as the Einstein equation are not (in and of themselves) FLOTEs that produce later states of the universe from earlier ones. For the same reason, PH, WCH, IPH, and NBWF cannot be Maudlinian laws. And neither can a purely spatial constraint such as Gauss's law[25] or the simple rule responsible for the Mandelbrot world. On MinP, they can all be understood as fundamental laws that express simple constraints.

The difficulty with dynamic production is not just that it precludes certain candidate fundamental laws. It is also difficult to understand the notion itself. What does dynamic production mean and what are its relata? Does it relate

---

[25] In personal communication, Maudlin suggests that he now regards (4) as expressing a metaphysical analysis or a definition of ρ in terms of the divergence of $\mathbf{E}$.

instantaneous states or sets of instantaneous states of the universe? If it relates instantaneous states, it is hard to understand dynamic production even in paradigm examples of FLOTEs such as the one expressed by Hamilton's equations. (The initial data is not confined to a single moment in time, if we understand momentum as partly reducible to variations in positions over some time interval.) The notion becomes even less natural in relativistic settings. Moreover, on a simple understanding of dynamic production, the beginning of the universe does metaphysical work; it is what gets the entire productive enterprise started. However, for spacetimes with no temporal boundaries, it is unclear where to start the productive explanation. In contrast, constraints operate on the entire spacetime, regardless of whether there is an "initial" moment. Thus, MinP does not require a first moment in time. (Perhaps a more sophisticated understanding of dynamic production does not either.)

On MinP, even if the universe lacks a fundamental direction of time, we can still recover a notion of productive explanation at a non-fundamental level. For example, we can use PH to define a (nonfundamental) direction of time in the usual way: *earlier* is defined as being closer to the time of PH, while *later* is defined as being further away from that. We may regard FLOTEs as evolving earlier states of the universe into later ones (with respect to PH). In such a universe, dynamic production may be metaphysically derivative. Still, we can contemplate a (non-fundamental) productive explanation of Bromberger's flagpole and vindicate the intuition that the pole length and the circumstances explain, but are not explained by, the shadow length. Therefore, the intuitive picture behind Maudlinian Primitivism can be preserved even if there is no fundamental notion of dynamic production or a fundamental direction of time.

4.6 Summary

We have surveyed five influential accounts of laws in the philosophical literature, and compared them with MinP. All four non-Humean accounts discussed here are more restrictive than MinP. Even though Humean Reductionism disagrees with MinP regarding the metaphysical status of laws, they agree on many first-order judgments about which equations express laws. This suggests that the fundamental disagreement between Humeanism and non-Humeanism is much more subtle than is often recognized.

5 Simplicity

Physical laws are strikingly simple, although there is no *a priori* reason they must be so. We have discussed the relevance of simplicity in Sections 3 and 4.1. Here we shall take a more systematic look at its role in the epistemology of laws. I propose that nomic realists of all types (Humeans and non-Humeans) should accept that simplicity is a fundamental epistemic guide for discovering and evaluating candidate laws. As it turns out, this epistemological principle is independent of the metaphysical posits about laws in both Humeanism and non-Humeanism.

5.1 Nomic Realism and the Epistemic Gap

Many physicists and philosophers are realists about physical laws. Call realism about physical laws *nomic realism*. It contains two parts:

Metaphysical Realism: Physical laws are objective and mind-independent; more precisely, which propositions express physical laws are objective and mind-independent facts in the world.[26]

Epistemic Realism: We have epistemic access to physical laws; more precisely, we can be epistemically justified in believing which propositions express the physical laws, given the evidence that we will in fact obtain.[27]

Nomic realism gives rise to an apparent epistemic gap: if laws are really objective and mind-independent, it may be puzzling how we can have epistemic access to them, since laws are not consequences of our observations. The epistemic gap can be seen as an instance of a more general one regarding theoretical statements on scientific realism (Chakravartty 2017).

The accounts surveyed in Sections 3 and 4 all aspire to satisfy nomic realism. Let us focus on BSA and MinP, as representatives of Humeanism and non-Humeanism. Do they vindicate epistemic realism? Their metaphysical posits, by themselves, do not guarantee epistemic realism. This should be clear on MinP. Since there is no metaphysical restriction on the form of the fundamental laws, if they are entirely mind-independent primitive facts about the world, how do we know which propositions are the laws? In fact, an analogous problem exists on BSA. This claim may surprise some philosophers, as it is often thought that BSA has an epistemic advantage over non-Humean accounts like MinP,

---

[26] A weaker version of metaphysical realism maintains that laws are not entirely mind-dependent. That will accommodate more pragmatic versions of the Humean best-system accounts (e.g. Loewer (2007b), Cohen and Callender (2009), Hicks (2018), Dorst (2019), Jaag and Loew (2020), and the volume edited by Hicks et al. (2023)), since on such views the mosaic still partially determines the best system. The arguments below should apply with suitable adaptations.

[27] The terminology is due to Earman and Roberts (2005). Here I've added the clause "given the evidence that we will in fact obtain." My version of epistemic realism is logically stronger than theirs, since theirs refers to all possible evidence we can obtain.

precisely because BSA brings laws closer to us. BSA defines laws in terms of the mosaic, and the mosaic is all we can empirically access (Earman and Roberts 2005).

The problem is that *we are not given the mosaic*. Just like laws, the mosaic entertained in modern physics is a theoretical entity that is not entailed by our observations. Our beliefs about its precise nature, such as the global structure of spacetime, its microscopic constituents, and the exact matter distribution, are as theoretical and inferential as our beliefs about laws. They are all parts of a theory about the physical world. Just as MinP requires an extra epistemic principle to infer what the laws are, BSA requires a similar principle to infer what the mosaic is like. The latter, on BSA, turns out to be equivalent to a strong epistemic principle concerning what we should expect about the best system given *our limited evidence*, which because of its limitation pins down neither the mosaic nor the best system. (See (Hildebrand 2022, Section 8) for a similar perspective; see also (Chen and Goldstein 2022, Section 4.1).)

After all, on BSA laws are not summaries of our observations only, but of the entire spacetime mosaic constituted by the totality of microphysical facts, a small minority of which show up in our observations. The ultimate judge of which system of propositions is the optimal true summary depends on the entire mosaic, a theoretical entity. (For this reason, BSA should not be confused as a version of strict empiricism.) And in current physics, our best guide to the mosaic is our best guess about the laws. At the end of the day, MinP and BSA turn out to require the same epistemic principle concerning laws. On neither account does the epistemic principle follow from the metaphysical posits about what laws are.

To sharpen the discussion, let us suppose, granting Lewis's assumption of the kindness of nature (Lewis 1994, p.479), that given the mosaic ξ there is a unique best system whose axioms express the fundamental law L:

$$L = BS(\xi) \tag{11}$$

with $BS(\cdot)$ the function that maps a mosaic to its best-system law.[28] Let us stipulate that for both BSA and MinP, physical reality is described by a pair (L, ξ). For both, we must have that $\xi \in \Omega^L$, with Ω^L the set of mosaics compatible with L. This means that L is true in ξ. On BSA, we also have that $L = BS(\xi)$. So in a sense, all we need in BSA is ξ; L is not ontologically extra. But it does not follow that BSA and MinP are relevantly different when it comes to epistemic realism.

---

[28] We might understand pragmatic Humeanism as recommending that we use another best-system function $BS'(\cdot)$ that is "best for us."

Let E denote our empirical evidence consisting of our observational data about physical reality. Let us be generous and allow E to include not just our current data but also all past and future data about the universe that we in fact gather. There are two salient features of E:

- E does not pin down a unique ξ. There are different candidates of ξ that yield the same E. (After all, E is a spatiotemporally partial and macroscopically coarse-grained description of ξ.)
- E does not pin down a unique L. There are different candidates of L that yield the same E. (On BSA, this is an instance of the previous point; on MinP, this is easier to see since L can vary independently of ξ, up to a point.)

Hence, on BSA, just as on MinP, E does not pin down (L, ξ). There is a gap between what our evidence entails and what the laws are. Ultimately, the gap can be bridged by adopting simplicity (among other theoretical virtues) as an epistemic guide. Nevertheless, it helps to see how big the gap is so that we can appreciate how much work needs to be done by simplicity and other epistemic guides.[29]

The epistemic gaps can be illustrated by considering cases of empirical equivalence. If different laws yield the same evidence, it is puzzling how we can be epistemically justified in choosing one over its empirically equivalent rivals, unless we rule them out by positing substantive assumptions that go beyond the metaphysical posits of nomic realism. Here I briefly mention three kinds of algorithms for generating empirical equivalents. For a more in-depth discussion, see Chen (2023c).

Algorithm A: Moving parts of ontology (what there is in the mosaic) into the nomology (the package of laws).

General strategy. This strategy works on both BSA and MinP. Given a theory of physical reality $T_1 = (L, \xi)$, if ξ can be decomposed into two parts $\xi_1 \& \xi_2$, we can construct an empirically equivalent rival $T_2 = (L \& \xi_1, \xi_2)$, where ξ_1 is moved from ontology to nomology.

---

[29] It is worth contrasting the current setup with the influential framework suggested by Hall (2009, 2015). To articulate a core idea of BSA, Hall imagines a Limited Oracular Perfect Physicist (LOPP) who has as her evidence all of ξ and nothing else. Her evidence E_{LOPP} contains vastly more information than E. On BSA, E_{LOPP} pins down (L, ξ). Actually, this is still incorrect. On BSA, we also need the assumption that E_{LOPP} corresponds to the entire spacetime, and the mosaic does not "continue" beyond E_{LOPP}. This subtlety has not been sufficiently appreciated in the literature. Notice that E_{LOPP} is as theoretical for Humeans as for non-Humeans. The Humean's best guess about what is in E_{LOPP} depends on her expectation about what L looks like given E.

Example. Consider the standard theory of Maxwellian electrodynamics, T_{M1}:

- Nomology: Maxwell's equations, Lorentz force law, and Newton's law of motion.
- Ontology: a Minkowski spacetime occupied by charged particles with trajectories $Q(t)$ and an electromagnetic field $F(x,t)$.

Here is an empirically equivalent rival, T_{M2}:

- Nomology: Maxwell's equations, Lorentz force law, Newton's law of motion, and an enormously complicated law specifying the exact functional form of $F(x,t)$ that appears in the dynamical equations.
- Ontology: a Minkowski spacetime occupied by charged particles with trajectories $Q(t)$.

Our evidence E is compatible with both T_{M1} and T_{M2}. The outcome of every experiment in the actual world will be consistent with T_{M2}, as long as the outcome is registered as certain macroscopic configuration of particles (Bell 2004). We can think of the new law in T_{M2} as akin to the Hamiltonian function in classical mechanics, which is interpreted as encoding all the classical force laws, except that specifying $F(x,t)$ is much more complicated than specifying a typical Hamiltonian. Both $F(x,t)$ and the Hamiltonian are components of respective laws of nature that tell particles how to move.[30] Given metaphysical realism, at most one of the two theories has the correct nomology.

Algorithm B: Changing the nomology directly.

General strategy. This strategy is designed for MinP. We can generate empirical equivalence by directly changing the nomology. Suppose the actual mosaic ξ is governed by the law L_1. Consider L_2, where $\Omega^{L_1} \neq \Omega^{L_2}$ and $\xi \in \Omega^{L_2}$. L_1 and L_2 are distinct laws because they have distinct sets of models. Since E (which can be regarded as a coarse-grained and partial description of ξ) can arise from both, the two laws are empirically equivalent. There are infinitely many such candidates for Ω^{L_2}. For example, Ω^{L_2} can be obtained by replacing one mosaic in Ω^{L_1} with something different and not already a member of Ω^{L_1}, by adding

---

[30] Note that we can decompose the standard ontology in many other dimensions, corresponding to more ways to generate empirically equivalent laws for a Maxwellian world. This move is discussed at length by Albert (2022). Similar strategies have been considered in the "quantum Humeanism" literature. See Miller (2014), Esfeld (2014), Callender (2015), Bhogal and Perry (2017), and Chen (2022a).

some mosaics to Ω^{L_1}, or by removing some mosaics in Ω^{L_1}. L_2 is empirically equivalent with L_1 since E is compatible with both.[31]

Example. Let L_1 be the Einstein equation of general relativity, with $\Omega^{L_1} = \Omega^{GR}$, the set of general relativistic spacetimes. Assume that the actual spacetime is governed by L_1, so that $\xi \in \Omega^{L_1}$. Consider L_2, a law that permits only the actual spacetime and completely specifies its microscopic detail, with $\Omega^{L_2} = \{\xi\}$. Since our evidence E arises from ξ, it is compatible with both L_1 and L_2. Since it needs to encode the exact detail of ξ, in general L_2 is much more complicated than L_1.[32] Given metaphysical realism, at most one of L_1 and L_2 corresponds to the actual law.

Algorithm C: Changing the nomology by changing the ontology.

General strategy. This strategy is designed for BSA. On BSA, we can change the nomology by making suitable changes in the ontology (mosaic), which will in general change what the best system is. Suppose the actual mosaic ξ is optimally described by the actual best system $L_1 = BS(\xi)$. We can consider a slightly different mosaic ξ', such that it differs from ξ in some spatiotemporal region that is never observed and yet E is compatible with both ξ and ξ'. There are infinitely many such candidates for ξ' whose best system $L_2 = BS(\xi')$ differs from L_1. Alternatively, we can expand ξ to $\xi' \neq \xi$ such that ξ is a proper part of ξ'. There are many such candidates for ξ' whose best system $L_2 = BS(\xi')$ differs from L_1, even though E is compatible with all of them.

Example. Let L_1 be the Einstein equation of general relativity, with $\Omega^{L_1} = \Omega^{GR}$, the set of general relativistic spacetimes. Assume that the actual spacetime is globally hyperbolic and optimally described by L_1, so that $L_1 = BS(\xi)$. Consider ξ', which differs from ξ in only the number of particles in a small spacetime region R in a far away galaxy that no direct observation is ever made. Since the number of particles is an invariant property of general relativity, it is left unchanged after a "hole transformation" (Norton 2019). We can use determinism to deduce that ξ' is incompatible with general relativity, so that $L_1 \neq BS(\xi')$. Let L_2 denote $BS(\xi')$. $L_1 \neq L_2$ and yet they are compatible with the same evidence we obtain in ξ. Since ξ' violates the conservation of number of particles, L_2 should be more complicated than L_1. Given metaphysical realism, at most one of L_1 and L_2 corresponds to the actual law.

Algorithms A, B, and C can be combined to generate more sophisticated cases of empirical equivalence. The question they raise is this: what breaks the tie among empirical equivalents and epistemically justifies our belief in the

---

[31] See Manchak (2009, 2020) for more examples.

[32] L_2 is a case of strong determinism; see Section 2.4.

intuitively correct law, given the evidence that we will in fact obtain? In other words, in cases of empirical equivalence, how can we hold on to epistemic realism given our commitment to metaphysical realism? To do so, we need a tie breaker.

5.2 Nomic Simplicity

I propose that *simplicity is a fundamental epistemic guide to lawhood*. Roughly speaking, simpler candidates are more likely to be laws, all else being equal. It secures epistemic realism in cases of empirical equivalence where simplicity is the deciding factor. In particular, we should accept this principle:

Principle of Nomic Simplicity (PNS) Other things being equal, simpler propositions are more likely to be laws. More precisely, other things being equal, for two propositions L_1 and L_2, if $L_1 >_S L_2$, then $L[L_1] >_P L[L_2]$, where $>_S$ represents the comparative simplicity relation, $>_P$ represents the comparative probability relation, and $L[\cdot]$ denotes *is a law*, which is an operator that maps a proposition to one about lawhood.[33]

As a fundamental principle, PNS is not justified by anything else.[34] But what is special about PNS, and why not use the oft-cited principle of simplicity as below?

Principle of Simplicity (PS) Other things being equal, simpler propositions are more likely to be true. More precisely, other things being equal, for two propositions L_1 and L_2, if $L_1 >_S L_2$, then $L_1 >_P L_2$, where $>_S$ represents the

---

[33] For example, $L[F = ma]$ expresses the proposition that $F=ma$ *is a law*. The proposition $F=ma$ is what Lange (2009) calls a "sub-nomic proposition."

[34] Saying that simplicity is a fundamental epistemic guide to lawhood does not mean it is the only such guide. Recall that PNS contains the proviso "other things being equal." But sometimes other factors are not held equal, and we need to consider overall comparisons of theoretical virtues (epistemic guides) and their balance. Other theoretical virtues can also serve as epistemic guides for lawhood. For example, informativeness and naturalness are two such virtues. A simple equation that does not describe much or describe things in too gruesome manners is less likely to be a law. We can formulate a more general principle:

Principle of Nomic Virtues (PNV) For two propositions L_1 and L_2, if $L_1 >_O L_2$, then $L[L_1] >_P L[L_2]$, where $>_O$ represents the relation of overall comparison that takes into account all the theoretical virtues and their tradeoffs, of which of which $>_S$ is a contributing factor, $>_P$ represents the comparative probability relation, and $L[\cdot]$ denotes *is a law*, which is an operator that maps a proposition to one about lawhood.

What is overall better is a holistic matter, and it can involve trade-offs among the theoretical virtues such as simplicity, informativeness, and naturalness. PNV should be thought of as the more general epistemic principle than PNS. I shall mainly focus on PNS, but what I say below should carry over to PNV.

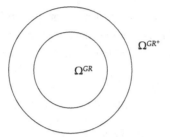

Figure 7 Ω^{GR} is nested within Ω^{GR^+}.

comparative simplicity relation, $>_P$ represents the comparative probability relation.[35]

The reason is that PS leads to probabilistic incoherence while PNS straight-forwardly avoids it. Whenever two theories have nested sets of models, say $\Omega^{L_1} \subset \Omega^{L_2}$, the probability that L_1 is true cannot be higher than the probability that L_2 is true. For concreteness, consider an example from spacetime physics. Let Ω^{GR} denote the set of models compatible with the fundamental law in general relativity – the Einstein equation, and let Ω^{GR^+} denote the union of Ω^{GR} and a few random spacetime models that do not satisfy the Einstein equation (see Figure 7). Suppose there is no simple law that generates Ω^{GR^+}. While the law of *GR* (the Einstein equation) is presumably simpler than that of *GR*$^+$, the former cannot be more likely to be true than the latter, since every model of *GR* is a model of *GR*$^+$, and not every model of *GR*$^+$ is a model of *GR*. This is an instance of the problem of nested theories, as Ω^{GR} is a subclass of and nested within Ω^{GR^+}.

On PS, in the case of nested theories, we have probabilistic incoherence. If L_1 is simpler than L_2, applying the principle that simpler laws are more likely to be true, we have $L_1 >_P L_2$. However, if L_1 and L_2 are nested with $\Omega^{L_1} \subset \Omega^{L_2}$, the axioms of probability entail that $L_1 \leq_P L_2$. Contradiction!

On PNS, we can avoid the problem. Even though we think that the Einstein equation is more likely to be a law, it is less likely to be true than the law of *GR*$^+$. According to PNS, what simplicity selects here is not truth in general, but truth about lawhood, that is whether a certain proposition has the property of being a fundamental law. Let us assume that fundamental lawhood is factive, which is granted on both BSA and MinP. Hence, lawhood implies truth: $L[p] \Rightarrow p$.

---

[35] It may be too demanding to require a total order that induces a *normalizable* probability distribution over the space of all possible laws. It is less demanding to formulate PS in terms of comparative probability.

However, truth does not imply lawhood: $p \nRightarrow L[p]$. This shows that $L[p]$ is logically inequivalent to p. This is the key to solve the problem of coherence.

On PNS, the contradiction that inflicts PS is removed, because *more likely to be a law* does not entail *more likely to be true*. If L_1 and L_2 are nested, where L_1 is simpler than L_2 but $\Omega^{L_1} \subset \Omega^{L_2}$, then $L_1 \leq_P L_2$. It is compatible with the fact that $L[L_1] >_P L[L_2]$. What we have is an inequality chain:

$$L[L_2] <_P L[L_1] \leq_P L_1 \leq_P L_2 \tag{12}$$

From the perspective of nomic realism, one can consistently endorse PNS without endorsing PS. Some facts are laws, but not all facts are laws. Laws correspond to a special set of facts. On BSA, they are the best-system axioms. On MinP, they are the primitive facts that constrain physical possibilities.

This is a simple solution to the problem of nested theories / problem of coherence, one that is suitable for both BSA and MinP.[36]

5.3 Theoretical Benefits

We should accept PNS because of its theoretical benefits. Here I highlight six attractive consequences of PNS.

Empirical equivalence. PNS is useful for resolving cases of empirical equivalence constructed along Algorithms A-C. For Algorithm A, T_2 will in general employ much more complicated laws than T_1. For example, the laws of T_{M2} specify $F(x, t)$ in its exact detail. For Algorithm B, L_2 will in general be more complicated than L_1, if Ω^{L_2} is obtained from Ω^{L_1} by adding or subtracting a few models. For example, a strongly deterministic theory of some sufficiently complex general relativistic spacetime, as described in the example, needs to specify the exact detail of that spacetime, will employ laws much more complicated than the Einstein equation. For Algorithm C, even though the mosaics of L_1 and L_2 are not that different, if L_1 is a simple system, then in general L_2 will not be. In fact, given enough changes from the actual mosaic, there may not be any optimal system that simplifies the altered mosaic to produce a good system. With PNS, we are justified in choosing the theoretical package with simpler laws, which agrees with standard theory choice.

Reflecting on our judgments in such cases, we may conclude that PNS is one posit we should make to justify epistemic realism about laws. It is what we presuppose when we set aside (or give less credence to) those empirical equivalents as epistemically irrelevant. As such, *it is not merely a pragmatic*

---

[36] It can be generalized to comparisons of laws that do not have nested sets of models (Chen 2023c). My solution in the context of laws is, in some aspect, similar to the solution proposed by Henderson (2023) in terms of a "generative view" of scientific theories.

principle, although it may have pragmatic benefits. Simpler laws may be easier to conceive, manipulate, falsify, and the like. But if it is an epistemic guide, it is ultimately aiming at certain truths about lawhood and providing epistemic justifications for our believing in such truths. There is, to be sure, the option of retreating from epistemic realism. But it is not open to nomic realists.

Induction. We want to know what the physical reality (L, ξ) is like. Given our limited evidence about some part of ξ and some aspect of L, what justifies our inference to other parts of ξ or other aspects of L that will be revealed in upcoming observations or in observations that could have been performed? It does not follow logically. Without some *a priori* rational guide to what (L, ξ) is like or probably like, we have no rational justification for favoring (L, ξ) over any alternative compatible with our limited evidence. On a given L we know what kind of ξ to expect. But we are given neither L or ξ. Without further inferential principles, it is hard to make sense of the viability of induction.

In Section 2.6, we discussed the potential connection between laws and induction. What does induction require of laws? One might demand that laws hold the same way everywhere and everywhen, but that is either vacuous or too inflexible. A better answer is the simplicity of laws, as required by PNS. A simple law can give rise to a complicated mosaic with an intricate matter distribution. The complexity is only apparent, because behind all the surface phenomena is a simple law that is discoverable. By assuming that the universe is governed by a simple law, one may make reasonable guesses about unobserved parts of the universe, based on a simple rule compatible with observed data. But nomic simplicity does not forbid laws about boundary conditions or about particular individuals. Some simple laws may even have temporal variations, such as a time-dependent function $F = \frac{1}{t+k} ma$ for some constant k. As long as the temporal variation and spatial variation are not too extreme as to require complicated laws, we can still inductively learn about physical reality based on available evidence, even in a non-uniform spacetime with dramatically different events in different regions.

In my view, a compelling argument that PNS is a *fundamental* epistemic principle can be made by its vindication of induction. The rationality of inductively learning about physical reality is indispensable to scientific practice and nomic realism. We can make a transcendental argument: science presupposes induction, so we have to believe in the epistemic rationality of induction. If Hume is right, induction has no noncircular epistemic justification. Deductive and probabilistic justifications of induction require premises that can be learnt only through induction. Therefore, whatever justification we offer for induction cannot completely satisfy the skeptic. We have to start somewhere by postulating fundamental epistemic principles that clarify how and why induction works.

Symmetry. Symmetry principles play important roles in theory construction and discovery. Physicists routinely use symmetries to justify or guide their physical postulates. However, whether symmetries hold is an empirical fact, not guaranteed by the world *a priori*. So why should we regard symmetry principles as useful, and what are they targeting? I suggest that certain applications of symmetry principles are defeasible guides for finding simple laws. In such cases, they are epistemically useful to the extent they are defeasible indicators for simplicity.[37] Consider the toy example

$$F = ma \text{ for } (-\infty, t] \text{ and } F = \left(8m^9 - \frac{1}{7}m^5 + \pi m^3 + km^2 + m\right) a \text{ for } (t, \infty) \tag{13}$$

with F given by Newtonian gravitation. This law violates time-translation invariance and time-reversal invariance. In this case, we have a much better law that is time-translation and time-reversal invariant:

$$F = ma \text{ for all times} \tag{14}$$

The presence of the two symmetries in (14) and the lack of them in (13), indicate that all else being equal we should prefer (14) to (13). We can explain this preference by appealing to their relative complexity. Equation (14) is much simpler than (13), and the existence of the symmetries are good indicators of the relative simplicity. However, in this comparison, we are assuming that both equations are valid for the relevant evidence (evidence obtained so far or total evidence that will ever be obtained). The preference is compatible with the fact that *if* empirical data is better captured by (13), we should prefer (13) to (14).

In the relevant situations where symmetry principles are guides to simplicity, they are only defeasible guides. Symmetry principles are not an end in itself for theory choice. I shall provide two more examples to show that familiar symmetry principles are not sacred and can be ultimately sacrificed if we already have a reasonably simple theory that is better than the alternatives.

The first is the toy example of the Mandelbrot world (Section 3.2). The physical reality consisting of (L_M, ξ_M) is friendly to scientific discovery. If we were inhabitants in that world, we can learn the structure of the whole ξ_M from the structure of its parts, by learning what L_M is. However, L_M is not a law with

---

[37] For a related perspective, see North (2021).

any recognizable spatial or temporal symmetries.[38] Nevertheless, the physical reality described by (L_M, ξ_M) is a perfect example of an ultimate theory (though not of the actual world). It is an elegant and powerful explanation for the patterns in the Mandelbrot world. What could be a better explanation? I suggest that none would be, even if it had more symmetries. In this case, we do not need symmetry principles to choose the right law, because we already have a simple and good candidate law. The lack of symmetries is not a regrettable feature of the world, but a consequence of its simple law.

The second and more realistic example is the Bohmian Wentaculus (Chen 2021a, 2022a, 2023d). With the Initial Projection Hypothesis (§3.3.2), the initial quantum state is as simple as the Past Hypothesis. This allows us to adopt the nomic interpretation of the quantum state, and understand the mosaic ξ_B as consisting of only particle trajectories in spacetime, with the fundamental dynamical law L_B as given by this differential equation:

$$\frac{dQ_i}{dt} = \frac{\hbar}{m_i} \mathrm{Im} \frac{\nabla_{q_i} W_{IPH}(q, q', t)}{W_{IPH}(q, q', t)} (Q)$$

$$= \frac{\hbar}{m_i} \mathrm{Im} \frac{\nabla_{q_i} \langle q| e^{-i\hat{H}t/\hbar} \hat{W}_{IPH}(t_0) e^{i\hat{H}t/\hbar} |q'\rangle}{\langle q| e^{-i\hat{H}t/\hbar} \hat{W}_{IPH}(t_0) e^{i\hat{H}t/\hbar} |q'\rangle} (q = q' = Q) \qquad (15)$$

Since the quantum state is nomic, as specified by a law, the right hand side should be the canonical formulation of the fundamental dynamical law for this world. Notice that the right hand side of the equation is not time-translation invariant, as at different times the expression

$$\mathrm{Im} \frac{\nabla_{q_i} \langle q| e^{-i\hat{H}t/\hbar} \hat{W}_{IPH}(t_0) e^{i\hat{H}t/\hbar} |q'\rangle}{\langle q| e^{-i\hat{H}t/\hbar} \hat{W}_{IPH}(t_0) e^{i\hat{H}t/\hbar} |q'\rangle}$$

will in general take on different forms. However, the physical reality described by the Bohmian Wentaculus may be our world, and the equation can be discovered scientifically. The law is a version of the Bohmian guidance equation that directly incorporates a version of the Past Hypothesis. Hence, (L_B, ξ_B) describes a physical reality that is friendly to scientific discovery and yet does not validate time-translation invariance.

In the Bohmian Wentaculus world, symmetry principles can be applied, but the fundamental dynamical law explicitly violates time-translation invariance. In such cases, the lack of symmetries is not a problem, because we already have found the simple candidate that has the desirable features. Again, the time-translation non-invariance is a consequence of its simple law. PNS takes

---

[38] There is, however, the reflection symmetry about the real axis. But it does not play any useful role here, and we can just focus on the upper half of the Mandelbrot world if needed.

precedence over symmetry principles and are the deeper justification for theory choice.

Dynamics. We have good reasons to allow fundamental laws of boundary conditions. However, many boundary conditions are not suitable candidates for fundamental lawhood. Epistemic guides such as simplicity allow us to be selective in postulating boundary condition laws, and to give more weight to proposals that include dynamical laws.

The examples of good boundary condition laws have a common feature: they are simple to specify. Many boundary conditions contain a great deal of correlations, but only a select few are good candidates for fundamental laws, namely those that are also sufficiently simple. One may wonder why we choose the Past Hypothesis, a macroscopic description, over a precise microscopic initial condition of the universe. The answer is that the former is much simpler than the latter and is still sufficiently powerful to explain a variety of temporally asymmetric regularities. The simplicity of the boundary condition laws make it almost inevitable that we will have dynamical laws in addition to boundary condition laws. The scientific explanations of natural phenomena come from the combination of simple boundary conditions and dynamical laws. As such, dynamical laws have to carry a lot of information by themselves.

Determinism. Nomic realism is often accompanied with other reasonable expectations about laws. On MinP, given any mosaic ξ, there are many possible choices of L such that $\xi \in \Omega^L$ and mosaics do not cross in Ω^L. Here is an algorithm to generate some of them: construct a two-member set $\Omega^L = \{\alpha, \beta\}$ such that α and β agree at no time (or any Cauchy surface). Any law with such a domain meets the definition of determinism. As long as α is not a world where every logically possible state of the universe happens some time in the universe, it is plausible to think that there are many different choices of β that can ensure determinism. Without a further principle about what we should expect of L, determinism is too easy and almost trivial on MinP. On BSA, the problem is the opposite. It becomes too difficult and almost impossible for a world to be deterministic. Given the evidence E we have about the mosaic, even though E may be optimally summarized by a deterministic law L, it does not guarantee (or make likely, without further assumptions) that the entire mosaic is optimally summarized by a deterministic law L. Small "perturbations" somewhere in the mosaic can easily make its best system fail determinism.[39]

Hence, there is a question of what nomic realists should say that constitutes a principled reason to think that determinism is not completely trivial (on MinP) and not epistemically inaccessible (on BSA). With PNS, determinism is no

---

[39] See Builes (2022) for a related argument.

longer trivial on MinP. Given any mosaic ξ, even though there are many deterministic candidates compatible with and true at ξ. Not every mosaic will be compatible with a relatively simple law that is deterministic. The non-triviality of determinism on MinP is the fact that it is non-trivial to find a law that is simple and deterministic, as that is not guaranteed for every metaphysically possible mosaic. With PNS, determinism is no longer epistemically inaccessible on BSA. This follows from the more general principle that PNS gives us epistemic justification to hold beliefs about parts of the mosaic that we have not observed and will never observe. We are justified in believing that the best system of the actual mosaic is relatively simple, even though the actual evidence does not entail that. If the actual evidence can be optimally summarized by a deterministic law restricted to the actual evidence, we have epistemic justification to make inferences about regions that will not be observed – the entire mosaic, ξ, can be summarized by a simple law that happens to be deterministic.

Explanation. There is a strong connection between nomic realism and scientific explanation. The point of postulating laws, on BSA and on MinP, is to provide scientific explanations. However, not all candidate laws provide the same quality of explanation or same kind of explanation. Hence, on both versions of nomic realism, we might wonder if there is a principled reason to think that we will have a successful scientific explanation for all phenomena.

On MinP, explanations must relate to us (Section 3.2). Constraints, in and of themselves, do not always provide satisfying explanations. Many constraints are complicated and thus insufficient for understanding nature. For example, the constraint given by just $\Omega^L = \{\xi_M\}$, which requires a complete specification of the mosaic, is insufficient for understanding the Mandelbrot world. Knowing why there is a pattern requires more than knowing the exact distribution of matter. On MinP, many candidate laws can constrain the mosaic. But not all have the level of simplicity to provide illumination about the mosaic. With PNS, we expect the actual constraint to be relatively simple. The constraint given by the Mandelbrot law should be preferred to that given by $\Omega^L = \{\xi_M\}$. The simple law provides a successful explanation while the more complicated one does not.

On BSA, it is built in the notion of laws that they systematize the mosaic. However, whether there is a systematization that is simpler than the mosaic is a contingent matter, depending on the detailed, microscopic, and global structures of the mosaic. Not every mosaic supports a systematization that provides illumination in the sense of unifying the diverse phenomena in the mosaic. BSA only entails that the best system is no more complex than the exact specification of the mosaic. For example, some mosaics may support no better optimal summary than the exact specification of the mosaic itself. Hence, on BSA, having successful explanations is not automatic. It requires the mosaic to be favorable. On BSA, some mosaics are favorable: they support optimal summaries that are simpler than themselves and provide "Humean explanations" about the mosaic. In fact, in a sense, most mosaics are not favorable (Lazarovici 2020). There exist mosaics underdetermined by actual evidence that do not support any good summaries. Given the actual evidence, with PNS, we are epistemically justified in inferring that the actual best system is relatively simple such that it can provide a "Humean explanation" about the actual mosaic. In effect, we are expecting that the actual Humean mosaic is a favorable one that completely cooperates with our scientific methodology and is such that it can be unified in a reasonably simple best system.

5.4 Summary

I suggest that nomic realists accept the principle of nomic simplicity as an epistemic guide for discovering and evaluating candidate laws. It vindicates epistemic realism when there is empirical equivalence (at least in those cases discussed in Section 5.1), avoids probabilistic incoherence when there are nested theories, and supports realist commitments regarding induction, symmetries, dynamics, determinism, and explanation. With many theoretical benefits for only a small price, it is a great bargain.

6 Exactness

Another hallmark of laws is their exactness, in contrast to the pervasive vagueness we find in ordinary language. A good way to understand something is to study its opposite. In this section, I discuss a model of nomic vagueness and a case study.

6.1 Nomic Exactness

Many predicates we use in everyday contexts do not have determinate boundaries of application. Is John bald when he has exactly 5250 hairs on his head? There are determinate cases of "bald," but there are also borderline cases of "bald." In other words, predicates such as "bald" are indeterminate: there are individuals such that it is indeterminate whether they are bald.[40] Moreover, the boundaries between "bald" and "borderline bald" are also indeterminate. There do not seem to be sharp boundaries *anywhere*, a phenomenon known as

---

[40] There are subtleties about how best to characterize vagueness. For reviews on vagueness and the sorites, see Keefe and Smith (1996), Sorensen (2018), and Hyde and Raffman (2018).

higher-order vagueness. Vagueness gives rise to many paradoxes (such as the sorites) and serious challenges to classical logic.

We might expect that, at the level of fundamental physics, the kind of vagueness that "infects" ordinary language should disappear. That is, the fundamental laws of physics, the predicates they invoke, and the properties they refer to should be exact. The expectation is supported by the history of physics and the ideal that physics should deliver an objective and precise description of nature. All the paradigm cases of candidate fundamental laws of nature are not only simple and universal, but also *exact*, in the sense that, for every class of worlds, fundamental laws either determinately apply or determinately fail. Suppose the fundamental laws are Newton's equation of motion $F = ma$ and law of universal gravitation $F = Gm_1m_2/r^2$: there is no vagueness about whether a physical history satisfies the laws. In other words, nomologically possible worlds form a set.

Fundamental nomic exactness – the ideal (roughly) that fundamental laws are exact – supports an important principle about the mathematical expressibility of fundamental laws. If some fundamental laws are vague, it will be difficult to describe them mathematically in a way that genuinely respects their vagueness and does not impose sharp boundaries anywhere. The kind of mathematics we are used to, built from a set-theoretic foundation, does not lend itself naturally to model the genuine fuzziness of vagueness. One could go further: the language of mathematics and the language of fundamental physics are supposed to be exemplars for the "ideal language," a language that is exact, suggested in Frege's *Begriffsschrift*, Russell's logical atomism, and Leibniz's *characteristica universalis*. The successful application of mathematical equations in formulating laws *seems* to leave no room for vagueness to enter into a fundamental physical theory. If there is fundamental nomic vagueness, and if vagueness is not completely mathematically expressible, then the fundamental physical theory is not completely mathematically expressible.

6.2 Nomic Vagueness

How should we understand the exactness of paradigm fundamental laws of nature? Let us start with the familiar case of Newtonian mechanics (with Newtonian gravitation). Its laws can be expressed as a set of differential equations that admit a determinate set of solutions. Those solutions specify all and only the possible histories compatible with the laws; each solution represents a nomologically possible world of the theory.

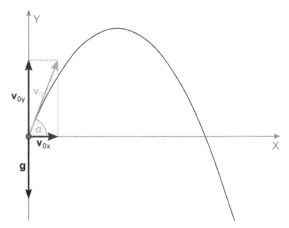

Figure 8 The motion of a projectile in Newtonian mechanics. Picture from Zátonyi Sándor, (ifj.) Fizped, CC BY-SA 3.0 <https://creativecommons.org/licenses/by-sa/3.0>, via Wikimedia Commons

Consider the projectile motion illustrated in Figure 8. Suppose that the projectile has unit mass m and the gravitational acceleration is g. We can specify the history of the projectile with the initial height, initial velocity, maximum height, and distance traveled. There is a set of histories compatible with the laws. For any history of the projectile, it is either determinately compatible with the equations or determinately incompatible with the equations.

If W represents the space of all possible worlds, then the nomologically possible worlds of Newtonian mechanics corresponds to Ω^{NM}, a proper subset in W that has a determinate boundary, where the boundary is not in spacetime but in modal space. For any possible world $w \in W$, either w is contained in Ω^{NM} or it is not. For example, in Figure 9, $w1$ is inside but $w2$ is outside Ω^{N}. In other words, $w1$ is nomologically possible while $w2$ is nomologically impossible if Newtonian laws are true and fundamental. Call Ω^{NM} the *domain* of Newtonian mechanics. We can capture an aspect of fundamental nomic exactness as the exactness of the domain:

Domain Exactness A fundamental law L is domain-exact if and only if, (a) for any world $w \in W$, there is a determinate fact about whether w is contained inside L's domain of worlds, that is L's domain has no borderline worlds, (b) L's domain, which may also be called L's *extension*, forms a set of worlds, (c) L's domain is not susceptible to sorites paradoxes, and (d) L's domain has no borderline borderline worlds, no borderline borderline borderline worlds, and so on.

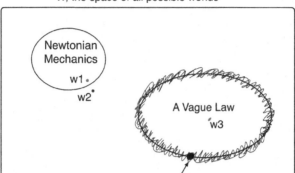

Figure 9 An exact fundamental law and a vague fundamental law represented in modal space.

In contrast, a domain-vague law has none of (a)–(d). Intuitively, a domain-vague law has a vague boundary in the following sense. In Figure 9, a domain-vague law is pictured by a "collection" of worlds with a fuzzy boundary. Just as a cloud does not have a clear starting point or a clear end point, the fuzzy "collection" of worlds does not delineate the worlds into those that are clearly compatible and those that are clearly incompatible with the law. To borrow the words of Sainsbury (1990), a domain-vague law classifies worlds "without setting boundaries" in modal space. For example, $w3$ is clearly contained inside the domain of the vague law, since it is so far away from the fuzzy boundary; but $w4$ is not clearly contained inside the domain of the vague law, and neither is it clearly outside; $w2$ is clearly outside the domain. More precisely, I propose that we understand domain vagueness as the opposite of domain exactness:

Domain Vagueness A fundamental law L is domain-vague if and only if L meets all four conditions below.

(a′) L has borderline worlds that are not determinately compatible with it. For some world $w \in W$, there fails to be a determinate fact about whether w is contained inside L's domain of worlds.

(b′) L lacks a well-defined extension in terms of a set of models or a set of nomological possibilities. Nomological necessities and possibilities turn out to be vague.

(c′) L is susceptible to sorites paradoxes. We can start from a world that is determinately lawful, proceed to gradually make small changes to the world along some relevant dimension, and eventually arrive at a world that is determinately unlawful. But no particular small change makes the difference between determinately lawful and determinately unlawful.

(d′) *L* possesses higher-order domain-vagueness. Whenever there are border-line lawful worlds, there are borderline borderline lawful worlds, and so on. It seems inappropriate to draw a sharp line anywhere. This reflects the genuine fuzziness of domain vagueness.

Domain vagueness has features similar to those of ordinary-language vagueness. Domain exactness and domain vagueness capture the kind of fundamental nomic exactness and fundamental nomic vagueness we are most interested in here. (There is another kind of fundamental nomic vagueness that results from vague objective probabilities or typicalities. See Goldstein (2012). Fenton-Glynn (2019) offers an account of imprecise (but not vague) chances in the best-system theory.)

6.3 A Case Study

The Past Hypothesis (PH) presents a case of fundamental nomic vagueness. To begin, we review some reasons for taking PH to be a candidate fundamental law. Given its role in explaining the Second Law of Thermodynamics, we have good reasons to take PH to be a law of nature. If PH is logically independent from other fundamental laws, such as the dynamical laws of temporal evolution, it cannot be derived from other fundamental laws. Hence, PH fails the necessary condition for non-fundamental laws (Section 2.7) and has to be a fundamental law.[41]

To see the vagueness of PH, we will examine several versions of PH. Here is one version of PH that is sometimes proposed:

Super Weak Past Hypothesis (SWPH) At one temporal boundary of space-time, the universe has very low entropy.

SWPH is obviously vague. How low is low? The collection of worlds with "low-entropy" initial conditions has fuzzy boundaries in the space of possible worlds. Hence, if SWPH were a fundamental law, then we would have domain vagueness.

However, SWPH may not be detailed enough to explain all the temporal asymmetries. For example, in order to explain the temporal asymmetries

---

[41] For more discussions about the lawful status of PH, see Albert (2000, 2015), Callender (2004), Loewer (2007a), and Chen (2022b, 2023a).

of records, intervention, and knowledge, Albert (2000) and Loewer (2020b) suggest that we need a more specific condition that narrows down the initial microstates to a particular macrostate. One way to specify the macrostate invokes exact numeral values for the macroscopic variables of the early universe. Let S_0, T_0, V_0, D_0 represent the exact values (or exact distributions) of (low) entropy, (high) temperature, (small) volume, and (roughly uniform) density distribution of the initial state. Consider the following version of PH:

Weak Past Hypothesis (WPH) At one temporal boundary of space-time, the universe is in a particular macrostate M_0, specified by the macroscopic variables S_0, T_0, V_0, and D_0.

WPH is a stronger version of PH than SWPH. By picking out a particular (low-entropy) macrostate M_0 from many macrostates, WPH more severely constrains the initial state of the universe. WPH is also more precise than SWPH. (Some may even complain that the WPH is too strong and too precise.) Unfortunately, WPH is still vague. The collection of worlds compatible with WPH has fuzzy boundaries. If WPH were a fundamental law, then we would still have nomic (domain) vagueness: there are some worlds whose initial conditions are borderline cases of being in the macrostate M_0, specified by the macroscopic variables S_0, T_0, V_0, and D_0.

The vagueness of WPH is revealed when we connect the macroscopic variables to the microscopic ones. Which set of microstates realizes the macrostate M_0? There is hardly any sharp boundary between those that do and those that do not realize the macrostate. A macrostate, after all, is a coarse-grained description of the physical state. As with many cases of coarse-graining, there can be borderline cases. (The vagueness of macrostates is similar to the vagueness of "is bald" and "is a table.") In fact, a macrostate can be vague even when it is specified with precise values of the macro-variables. This point should be familiar to those working in the foundations of statistical mechanics.[42] However, it is worth spelling out the reasons to understand where and why such vagueness exists.

There is a systematic way to think about the vagueness of the thermodynamic macrostates in general and the vagueness of M_0 in the WPH. In the Boltzmannian account of classical statistical mechanics, macrostates and microstates can be understood as certain structures on phase space (Figure 10).

---

[42] Commenting on the vagueness of the macrostate boundaries, Loewer (2007a) writes, "Obviously, the notion of *macro state* is vague and there are many precisifications that would serve the purposes of statistical mechanics." Goldstein et al. (2020) write, "there is some arbitrariness in where exactly to 'draw the boundaries.'"

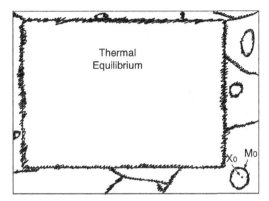

Figure 10 A diagram of phase space where macrostates have fuzzy boundaries. The macrostate M_0 represents the initial low-entropy condition described by WPH. X_0 is the actual initial microstate. The picture is not drawn to scale.

- Phase space: in classical mechanics, phase space is a 6N-dimensional space that encodes all the microscopic possibilities of the system.
- Microstate: a point in phase space, which is a maximally specific description of a system. In classical mechanics, the microstate specifies the positions and the momenta of all particles.
- Macrostate: a region in phase space in which the points inside are macroscopically similar, which is a less detailed and more coarse-grained description of a system. The largest macrostate is thermal equilibrium.
- Fuzziness: the partition of phase space into macrostates is not exact; the macrostates have fuzzy boundaries. Their boundaries become exact only given some choices of the "C-parameters," including the size of cells for coarse-graining and the correspondence between distribution functions and macroscopic variables.
- Entropy: $S(x) = k_B \log |M(x)|$, where $| \cdot |$ denotes the standard volume measure in phase space. Because of Fuzziness, in general, the (Boltzmann) entropy of a system is not exact.

We can translate WPH into the language of phase space: at one temporal boundary of space-time, the microstate of the universe X_0 lies inside a particular macrostate M_0 that has low volume in phase space.

Fuzziness is crucial for understanding the vagueness and higher-order vagueness of macrostates. Without specifying the exact values (or exact ranges of values) of the C-parameters, the macrostates have fuzzy boundaries: some microstates are borderline cases for certain macrostates, some are borderline borderline cases, and so on. The fuzzy boundary of M_0 illustrates the existence of borderline microstates and higher-order vagueness. There will be a precise identification of macrostates with sets of microstates only when we exactly specify the C-parameters (or their ranges). In other words, there is a precise partition of microstates on phase space into regions that are macroscopically similar (macrostates) only when we make some arbitrary choices about what the C-parameters are. In such situations, the WPH macrostate M_0 would correspond to an exact set Γ_0 on phase space, and the initial microstate has to be contained in Γ_0.

However, proponents of the WPH do not specify a precise set. A precise set Γ_0 would require more precision than is given in statistical mechanics – it requires the specific values of the coarse-grained cells and the specific correspondence with distribution functions. (In the standard quantum case, it also requires the precise cut-off threshold for when a superposition belongs to a macrostate.) The precise values of the C-parameters could be added to the theory to make WPH into a precise statement (which I call the *Strong Past Hypothesis* in Chen (2022b)). But they are nowhere to be found in the proposal, and rightly so.[43]

Some choices of the C-parameters are clearly unacceptable. If the coarse-graining cells are too large, they cannot reflect the variations in the values of macroscopic variables; if the coarse-graining cells are too small, they may not contain enough gas molecules to be statistically significant. Hence, they have to be macroscopically small but microscopically large (Albert (2000) p.44(fn.5) and Goldstein et al. (2020)). However, if we were to make the parameters (or the ranges of parameters) more and more precise, beyond a certain point, any extra precision in the choice would seem completely arbitrary. They correspond to how large the cells are and which function is the correct one when defining the relation between temperature and sets of microstates. That does not seem to correspond to any objective facts in the world. (How large is large enough and how small is small enough?) In this respect, the arbitrariness in precise C-parameters is quite unlike that in the fundamental dynamical constants. (In Chen (2022b), I discuss their differences in terms of a theoretical virtue called "traceability.") Moreover, not only do we lack precise parameters, we also lack a precise set of permissible parameters (hence no exact ranges of values for the C-parameters). There shouldn't be sharp boundaries anywhere. Suppose size m is borderline large enough and size n is determinately large enough. Small changes from m will eventually get us to n, but it is implausible that there is a sharp transition from borderline large enough to determinately large enough. Similarly, there

---

[43] For example, see descriptions of SWPH and WPH in Goldstein (2001), Albert (2000), and Carroll (2010).

shouldn't be a sharp transition between borderline large enough to borderline borderline large enough, and so on. That is higher-order vagueness.

Because of higher-order vagueness, we need to take standard mathematical representation of WPH with a grain of salt. The macroscopic variables – adjustable parameters in WPH – need to be coarse-grained enough to respect the vagueness. For example, we may *represent* the temperature of M_0 as 10^{32} degrees Kelvin. But temperature does not have the exactness of real numbers. A more careful way to represent the vague temperature should be "10^{32}-ish degrees Kelvin," where the "-ish" qualifier signifies that temperature is vague and the number 10^{32} is only an imperfect mathematical representation.[44] Its exactness is artificial. Hence, WPH should be characterized as a macrostate M_0 specified by S_0-ish entropy, T_0-ish temperature, and so on.

The vagueness here is appropriate, since macroscopic variables only make sense when there are enough degrees of freedom (such as a large number of particles). In practice, however, such vagueness rarely matters: there will be enough margins such that to explain the thermodynamic phenomena, which are themselves vague, we do not need the extra exactness. The vagueness disappears *for all practical purposes*. Nevertheless, WPH is a genuine case of fundamental nomic vagueness and it is a possibility to take seriously.

6.4 Summary

I have suggested that fundamental laws of physics can be vague, and PH provides an example. However, nomic vagueness may be an artifact of classical mechanics and can be naturally avoided in quantum mechanics (Chen 2022b, Sect. 4). Hence, nomic exactness may be a metaphysically contingent feature of the universe that depends on the actual laws.

7 Objectivity

The final hallmark of laws I want to discuss is their objectivity. Laws are objective features of reality that do not depend on our beliefs or desires. They are mind-independent. However, the metaphysics of laws can make a difference to how we understand their objectivity.

7.1 Ratbag Idealism

Humeanism and non-Humeanism offer different understandings about the objectivity of laws. Let us focus on BSA and MinP. On BSA, assuming that we are relying on the right theoretical virtues and have appropriate access to

---

[44] Thanks to Alan Hájek for discussions here.

the mosaic, the best summaries will be the true laws. There is a certain sense that, in principle, we are guaranteed to be right. On MinP, even if we rely on the correct theoretical virtues and the correct scientific methodology, we can still be mistaken about what the true laws are. Epistemic guides are defeasible and fallible indicators for truth: they do not guarantee that we find the true laws (although we may be rational to expect to find them). There are fundamental, objective, and mind-independent facts about which laws govern the world, and we can be wrong about them. This is not a bug but a feature of MinP, symptomatic of the robust kind of realism that we endorse. For realists, this is exactly where they should end up; fallibility about the fundamental reality is a badge of honor.

On BSA, since the best systematization is constitutive of lawhood, and what counts as best may depend on us, lawhood can become mind-dependent. In a passage about "ratbag idealism," Lewis (1994) discusses this worry and tries to offer a solution:

> The worst problem about the best-system analysis is that when we ask where the standards of simplicity and strength and balance come from, the answer may seem to be that they come from us. Now, some ratbag idealist might say that if we don't like the misfortunes that the laws of nature visit upon us, we can change the laws – in fact, we can make them always have been different – just by changing the way we think! (Talk about the power of positive thinking.) It would be very bad if my analysis endorsed such lunacy. . . .
>
> The real answer lies elsewhere: if nature is kind to us, the problem needn't arise. . . . If nature is kind, the best system will be *robustly* best – so far ahead of its rivals that it will come out first under any standards of simplicity and strength and balance. We have no guarantee that nature is kind in this way, but no evidence that it isn't. It's a reasonable hope. Perhaps we presuppose it in our thinking about law. I can admit that *if* nature were unkind, and *if* disagreeing rival systems were running neck-and-neck, then lawhood might be a psychological matter, and that would be very peculiar. (p.479)

For Lewis, the solution is conditionalized on the hope that nature is kind to us in this special way: the best summary of the mosaic will be far better than its rivals. That may be a generous assumption, but it seems consistent with scientific practice.

In contrast, the worry about ratbag idealism does not arise on MinP; the objectivity of laws can be secured without appealing to the hope that nature is kind to us. On MinP, fundamental laws are what they are irrespective of our psychology and judgments of simplicity and informativeness. Even though the epistemic guides provide some guidance for discovering and evaluating them, they do not guarantee arrival at the true fundamental laws. Moreover, changing our psychology or judgments will not change which facts are fundamental laws. Hence, MinP respects our conviction about the objectivity and mind-independence of fundamental laws.

7.2 A Package Deal

Despite the difference regarding the metaphysical objectivity of laws, there is a convergence in methodological principles underlying MinP and BSA, which may be traced back to epistemic principles that are somewhat mind-dependent. In Section 7.3, we discuss the epistemic version of ratbag idealism.

So far we have focused on fundamental laws. Fundamental laws are conceptually connected to fundamental ontology (fundamental material entities and their properties). On MinP, we regard both as metaphysical primitives and evaluate them in a package. In this respect, MinP is similar to Loewer's Package Deal Account (PDA), a descendent of BSA that regards both as co-equal elements of a package deal (Loewer 2020c, 2021), but they also have significant differences.

On PDA, we look for the best systematization in terms of a package of laws and (material) ontology; the package is supervenient on the actual world. Thus, fundamental laws and fundamental ontology enter the discussion in the same way, at the same place, and on the same level. MinP shares this feature, although fundamental ontology and fundamental laws are merely discovered by us and not made by us or dependent on us. On PDA, given the actual world (of which we have very limited knowledge), we evaluate different packages of laws + ontology, and we evaluate them based on our actual scientific practice. Hence, there will be some degree of relativism. Relative to different scientific practice or a different set of scientists, the judgement as to the actual laws + ontology would have been different. Consequently on PDA, fundamental laws and fundamental ontology are dependent on us in a significant way.

On MinP, we may use the best package-deal systematization as a guide to discover the laws and ontology; given the actual world (of which we have very limited knowledge), we evaluate different packages of laws + ontology, and we evaluate them based on our actual scientific practice. Hence, there will be some degree of uncertainty. Relative to different scientific practice or a different set of scientists, the judgement as to the actual laws + ontology would have been different. Still, what they are is metaphysically independent of our belief and practice.

Here I quote a passage from Loewer (2021). Although we disagree on the metaphysics, we agree on how the enterprise of physics should be understood:

> The best way of understanding the enterprise of physics is that it begins, as Quine says, "in the middle" with the investigation of the motions of macroscopic material objects e.g., planets, projectiles, pendula, pointers, and so on. Physics advances by proposing theories that include laws that explain the motions of macroscopic objects and their parts. These theories may (and often do) introduce ontology, properties/relations, and laws beyond macroscopic ones with which it began and go onto to posit laws that explain their behaviors. . . . . . The ultimate goal of this process is the discovery of a theory of everything (TOE) that specifies a fundamental ontology and fundamental laws that that cover not only the motions of macroscopic objects with which physics began but also whatever additional ontology and quantities that have been introduced along the way. (pp. 30–31)

From the perspective of MinP, this is an excellent description of how fundamental laws and ontology are discovered – in a package.

7.3 Humeanism and Non-Humeanism

Let us return to the problem of ratbag idealism. (Hall 2009, Section 5.6) suggests that, facing the problem that the simplicity criterion in the BSA is too subjective, Lewis and other Humeans can "perform a nifty judo move." If non-Humeans regard simplicity as an epistemic guide to laws, it follows that "central facts of normative epistemology are *also* up to us." Hall suggests that this is more objectionable than the ratbag idealism of BSA. A defender of BSA may reasonably embrace ratbag idealism and take laws to be pragmatic tools to structure our investigation of the world. With that viewpoint, we can expect that what laws are is somewhat up to us. However, there is no reason on non-Humeanism why fundamental epistemological and normative facts should be up to us. So the non-Humeans face a worse problem of ratbag idealism.

My analysis in Section 5 suggests that both Humeans and non-Humeans need to adopt fairly strong epistemological principles such as PNS. On Humeanism, there are two independent appeals to simplicity (among other theoretical virtues). The metaphysical analysis of laws with BSA requires laws be no more complicated than the mosaic. But not all mosaics support simple laws; in fact, many metaphysically possible mosaics may not have any regularity that deserves the label of laws. To believe, on BSA, that simple laws exist is to believe that the actual mosaic is very special. The epistemic guide to simple laws serves as an epistemic and normative restriction of possible candidate mosaics Humeans ought to consider. Why the Humean mosaic should be so nice on BSA is basically the same question as why fundamental constraints should be so simple on MinP. So on both BSA and MinP, epistemological and normative facts are up to us. Humeans cannot avoid the problem that "central facts of normative epistemology" may be up to us, unless they retreat to anti-realism about the mosaic. Insofar as they also need PNS, Humeans cannot perform the nifty judo move without undermining their own position.

Moreover, the analysis reveals a deeper difference between Humeanism and non-Humeanism. On MinP, we should assume (by PNS) that certain fundamental facts of the world are simple. In contrast, on BSA, we should assume (by PNS) that certain superficial facts of the world (best-system laws), grounded in a complex fundamental reality, are simple. The assumption on MinP, it seems to me, is more believable than the corresponding one on BSA. It is easier to believe that nature at some deep level is simple. It is harder to believe that nature at some deep level is complicated in a certain way to give rise to a simple appearance. Of course, this will not persuade the committed Humeans, for presumably they are willing to accept the consequence. However, for many people on the fence or coming to the debate for the first time, the choice between Humeanism and non-Humeanism should be clear.[45]

7.4 Summary

On non-Humeanism such as MinP, laws are objective. On Humeanism, in contrast, we need further assumptions about the mosaic to maintain their objectivity and to reject ratbag idealism. Insofar as there is an epistemic version of ratbag idealism concerning the objectivity of epistemic guides, it is not a special problem for non-Humeanism.

8 Conclusion

Laws occupy a central place in a systematic philosophy of the physical world. They can be regarded as fundamental facts that govern the universe by constraining its physical possibilities. With this minimal primitivist account, one accepts that laws transcend the concrete physical reality they govern, but need not presume a fundamental direction of time or require a fundamental ontology of universals, dispositions, or counterfactuals. The account allows one to contemplate a variety of candidate fundamental laws, and to understand the marks of the nomic as arising from methodological and epistemological principles. It is not the only viewpoint available, but it is one I recommend to anyone looking for an account that illuminates metaphysics but is not unduly constrained by it.

---

[45] See also Chen and Goldstein 2022 (pp.57–58). This argument requires more space to develop, which I leave to future work. I am indebted to discussions with Tyler Hildebrand and Boris Kment about this point.

In this Element, we have surveyed some of the considerations, concepts, and tools in philosophical discussions about laws and several issues regarding the metaphysics and the epistemology of laws. There are many more questions to explore, such as the following:

- What is a good criterion for determining when two laws are equivalent?
- How to develop a satisfactory account of probabilistic laws?
- How are laws of physics related to laws of the special sciences (insofar as the latter employ laws)?
- How should different accounts of laws inform theories of causation and counterfactuals?

I hope this Element has provided the readers with a philosophical foundation to continue thinking about laws of physics and the many topics they are connected to.

References

Adlam, E. (2022a). Determinism beyond time evolution. *European Journal for Philosophy of Science*, 12(4):73.

Adlam, E. (2022b). Laws of nature as constraints. *Foundations of Physics*, 52(1):28.

Albert, D. Z. (2000). *Time and Chance*. Harvard University Press.

Albert, D. Z. (2015). *After Physics*. Harvard University Press.

Albert, D. Z. (2022). Physical laws and physical things (manuscript).

Armstrong, D. M. (1983). *What Is a Law of Nature?* Cambridge University Press.

Arnowitt, R., Deser, S., and Misner, C. W. (1962). The dynamics of general relativity. In Witten, L., editor, *Gravitation: An Introduction to Current Research*, pages 227–264. New York: Wiley.

Ashtekar, A. and Gupt, B. (2016a). Initial conditions for cosmological perturbations. *Classical and Quantum Gravity*, 34(3):035004.

Ashtekar, A. and Gupt, B. (2016b). Quantum gravity in the sky: Interplay between fundamental theory and observations. *Classical and Quantum Gravity*, 34(1):014002.

Barrett, J. A. (1995). The distribution postulate in Bohm's theory. *Topoi*, 14(1):45–54.

Barrett, J. A. and Chen, E. K. (2023). Algorithmic randomness and probabilistic laws. *arXiv preprint:2303.01411*.

Beebee, H. (2000). The non-governing conception of laws of nature. *Philosophy and Phenomenological Research*, 61:571–594.

Bell, J. S. (2004). *Speakable and Unspeakable in Quantum Physics: Collected Papers on Quantum Philosophy*. Cambridge University Press.

Ben-Menahem, Y. (2018). *Causation in Science*. Princeton University Press.

Bhogal, H. (2017). Minimal anti-Humeanism. *Australasian Journal of Philosophy*, 95(3):447–460.

Bhogal, H. and Perry, Z. (2017). What the Humean should say about entanglement. *Noûs*, 51(1):74–94.

Bird, A. (2007). *Nature's Metaphysics: Laws and Properties*. Oxford University Press.

Buides, D. (2022). The ineffability of induction. *Philosophy and Phenomenological Research*, 104(1):129–149.

Callender, C. (2004). Measures, explanations and the past: Should "special" initial conditions be explained? *The British Journal for the Philosophy of Science*, 55(2):195–217.

Callender, C. (2015). One world, one beable. *Synthese*, 192(10):3153–3177.

Callender, C. (2017). *What Makes Time Special?* Oxford University Press.

Carroll, J. W. (1994). *Laws of Nature*. Cambridge University Press.

Carroll, J. W. (2018). Becoming Humean. In Ott, W. and Patton, L., editors, *Laws of Nature*, pages 122–138. Oxford University Press.

Carroll, S. (2010). *From Eternity to Here: The Quest for the Ultimate Theory of Time*. Penguin.

Cartwright, N. (1983). *How the Laws of Physics Lie*. Oxford University Press.

Cartwright, N. (1994). *Nature's Capacities and Their Measurement*. Oxford University Press.

Chakravartty, A. (2017). Scientific realism. In Zalta, E. N., editor, *The Stanford Encyclopedia of Philosophy*. Metaphysics Research Lab, Stanford University, Summer 2017 edition.

Chen, E. K. (2021a). Quantum mechanics in a time-asymmetric universe: On the nature of the initial quantum state. *The British Journal for the Philosophy of Science*, 72(4):1155–1183. doi.org/10.1093/bjps/axy068.

Chen, E. K. (2021b). The cosmic void. In Bernstein, S. and Goldschmidt, T., editors, *Non-being: New Essays on the Metaphysics of Nonexistence*, pages 115–138. Oxford University Press.

Chen, E. K. (2022a). From time asymmetry to quantum entanglement: The Humean unification. *Noûs*, 56:227–255.

Chen, E. K. (2022b). Fundamental nomic vagueness. *The Philosophical Review*, 131(1) 1–49.

Chen, E. K. (2022c). Strong determinism. *Philosophers' Imprint*, forthcoming, arXiv:2203.02886.

Chen, E. K. (2023a). The past hypothesis and the nature of physical laws. In Loewer, B., Eric Winsberg and Weslake, B., editors, *The Probability Map of the Universe: Essays on David Albert's Time and Chance*, pages 204–248. Harvard University Press.

Chen, E. K. (2023b). The preordained quantum universe. *Nature*, 624:513–515.

Chen, E. K. (2023c). The simplicity of physical laws. *arXiv preprint: 2210.08143*.

Chen, E. K. (2023d). The Wentaculus: Density matrix realism meets the arrow of time. In Bassi, A., Goldstein, S., Roderich Tumulka and Zanghì, N., editors, *Physics and the Nature of Reality: Essays in Memory of Detlef Dürr*. Springer, forthcoming.

Chen, E. K. and Goldstein, S. (2022). Governing without a fundamental direction of time: Minimal primitivism about laws of nature. In Ben-Menahem, Y., editor, *Rethinking the Concept of Law of Nature*, pages 21–64. Springer.

Choi, S. and Fara, M. (2021). Dispositions. In Zalta, E. N., editor, *The Stanford Encyclopedia of Philosophy*. Metaphysics Research Lab, Stanford University, Spring 2021 edition.

Cohen, J. and Callender, C. (2009). A better best system account of lawhood. *Philosophical Studies*, 145(1):1–34.

Deckert, D.-A. (2010). *Electrodynamic Absorber Theory: A Mathematical Study*. PhD thesis, Ludwig Maximilian University of Munich.

Demarest, H. (2017). Powerful properties, powerless laws. In Jacobs, J. D., editor, *Causal Powers*, pages 38–53. Oxford University Press Oxford.

Demarest, H. (2021). Powers, best systems, and explanation. *Manuscript*.

Dirac, P. A. (1937). The cosmological constants. *Nature*, 139(3512):323.

Dorst, C. (2019). Towards a best predictive system account of laws of nature. *The British Journal for the Philosophy of Science*, 70(3):877–900.

Dorst, C. (2023). Productive laws in relativistic spacetimes. *Philosophers' Imprint (forthcoming)*.

Dretske, F. (1977). Laws of nature. *Philosophy of Science*, 44:248–268.

Dürr, D., Goldstein, S., and Zanghì, N. (1992). Quantum equilibrium and the origin of absolute uncertainty. *Journal of Statistical Physics*, 67(5–6):843–907.

Earman, J. (1986). *A Primer on Determinism*, volume 32. D. Reidel.

Earman, J. and Roberts, J. T. (2005). Contact with the nomic: A challenge for deniers of Humean supervenience about laws of nature part II: The epistemological argument for Humean supervenience. *Philosophy and Phenomenological Research*, 71(2):253–286.

Elga, A. (2004). Infinitesimal chances and the laws of nature. *Australasian Journal of Philosophy*, 82(1):67–76.

Ellis, B. (2001). *Scientific Essentialism*. Cambridge University Press.

Ellis, B. (2014). *The Philosophy of Nature: A Guide to the New Essentialism*. Routledge.

Emery, N. (2019). Laws and their instances. *Philosophical Studies*, 176(6): 1535–1561.

Emery, N. (2023). *Naturalism Beyond the Limits of Science: How Scientific Methodology Can and Should Shape Philosophical Theorizing*. Oxford University Press.

Esfeld, M. (2014). Quantum Humeanism, or: Physicalism without properties. *The Philosophical Quarterly*, 64(256):453–470.

Fenton-Glynn, L. (2019). Imprecise chance and the best system analysis. *Philosophers' Imprint*, 19(23):1–44.

Fernandes, A. (2023). *The Temporal Asymmetry of Causation*. Cambridge University Press.

Foster, J. (2004). *The Divine Lawmaker: Lectures on Induction, Laws of Nature, and the Existence of God*. Clarendon Press.

Friederich, S. and Evans, P. W. (2019). Retrocausality in quantum mechanics. In Zalta, E. N., editor, *The Stanford Encyclopedia of Philosophy*. Metaphysics Research Lab, Stanford University, Summer 2019 edition.

Ghirardi, G. (2018). Collapse theories. In Zalta, E. N., editor, *The Stanford Encyclopedia of Philosophy*. Metaphysics Research Lab, Stanford University, Fall 2018 edition.

Ghirardi, G., Rimini, A., and Weber, T. (1986). Unified dynamics for microscopic and macroscopic systems. *Physical Review D*, 34(2):470.

Goldstein, S. (2001). Boltzmann's approach to statistical mechanics. In Bricmont, J., Dürr, D., Galavotti, M. C., et al., editors, *Chance in Physics*, pages 39–54. Springer.

Goldstein, S. (2012). Typicality and notions of probability in physics. In Yemima Ben-Menahem and Meir Hemmo, editors, *Probability in physics*, pages 59–71. Springer.

Goldstein, S. (2017). Bohmian mechanics. In Zalta, E. N., editor, *The Stanford Encyclopedia of Philosophy*. Metaphysics Research Lab, Stanford University, Summer 2017 edition.

Goldstein, S., Lebowitz, J. L., Tumulka, R., and Zanghì, N. (2020). Gibbs and Boltzmann entropy in classical and quantum mechanics. In Allori, V., editor, *Statistical Mechanics and Scientific Explanation: Determinism, Indeterminism and Laws of Nature*, pages 519–581. World Scientific.

Hall, N. (2004). Two concepts of causation. In Collins, J., Hall, N., and Paul, L., editors, *Causation and Counterfactuals*, pages 225–276. MIT Press.

Hall, N. (2009). Humean reductionism about laws of nature. *Manuscript*. http://philpapers.org/rec/HALHRA.

Hall, N. (2015). Humean reductionism about laws of nature. In Barry Loewer and Jonathan Schaffer, editors, *A companion to David Lewis*, pages 262–277. John Wiley & Sons.

Hartle, J. (1996). Scientific knowledge from the perspective of quantum cosmology. In John L. Casti and Anders Karlqvist, editors, *Boundaries and Barriers: On the Limits to Scientific Knowledge*. Addison-Wesley; arXiv:gr-qc/9601046.

Hartle, J. B. (1997). Quantum cosmology: Problems for the 21st century. In K. Kikkawa, Hiroshi Kunitomo, and H. Ohtsubo, editors, *Physics in the 21st century*, pages 179–199. World Scientific; arXiv:gr-qc/9701022.

Hartle, J. B. and Hawking, S. W. (1983). Wave function of the universe. *Physical Review D*, 28(12):2960–2975.

Henderson, L. (2022). The problem of induction. In Zalta, E. N. and Nodelman, U., editors, *The Stanford Encyclopedia of Philosophy*. Metaphysics Research Lab, Stanford University, Winter 2022 edition.

Henderson, L. (2023). On the mutual exclusivity of competing hypotheses. In Schupbach, J. N. and Glass, D. H., editors, *Conjunctive Explanations: The Nature, Epistemology, and Psychology of Explanatory Multiplicity*, pages 170–194. Routledge.

Hicks, M. T. (2018). Dynamic Humeanism. *The British Journal for the Philosophy of Science*, 69(4): 983–1007.

Hicks, M. T. and Schaer, J. (2017). Derivative properties in fundamental laws. *The British Journal for the Philosophy of Science*, 68(2):411–450.

Hicks, M. T., Jaag, S., and Loew, C., editors (2023). *Humean Laws for Humean Agents*. Oxford University Press.

Hildebrand, T. (2013). Can primitive laws explain? *Philosophers' Imprint*, 13:1–15.

Hildebrand, T. (2022). *Laws of Nature*. Cambridge University Press.

Hildebrand, T. and Metcalf, T. (2021). The nomological argument for the existence of God. *Noûs* 56(2):443–472.

Hitchcock, C. (2023). Causal Models. In Zalta, E. N. and Nodelman, U., editors, *The Stanford Encyclopedia of Philosophy*. Metaphysics Research Lab, Stanford University, Spring 2023 edition.

Hoefer, C. (2002). Freedom from the inside out. *Royal Institute of Philosophy Supplements*, 50:201–222.

Hoefer, C. (2016). Causal determinism. In Zalta, E. N., editor, *The Stanford Encyclopedia of Philosophy*. Metaphysics Research Lab, Stanford University, Spring 2016 edition.

Hyde, D. and Raffman, D. (2018). Sorites paradox. In Zalta, E. N., editor, *The Stanford Encyclopedia of Philosophy*. Metaphysics Research Lab, Stanford University, Summer 2018 edition.

Ismael, J. (2016). *How Physics Makes Us Free*. Oxford University Press.

Ismael, J. T. (2009). Probability in deterministic physics. *The Journal of Philosophy*, 106(2):89–108.

Jaag, S. and Loew, C. (2020). Making best systems best for us. *Synthese*, 197:2525–2550.

Keefe, R. and Smith, P. (1996). Introduction. In Keefe, R. and Smith, P., editors, *Vagueness: A Reader*, pages 1–57. MIT Press.

Kimpton-Nye, S. (2017). Humean laws in an unHumean world. *Journal of the American Philosophical Association*, 3(2):129–147.

Kraut, R. (2017). Plato. In Zalta, E. N., editor, *The Stanford Encyclopedia of Philosophy*. Metaphysics Research Lab, Stanford University, Fall 2017 edition.

Kutach, D. N. (2002). The entropy theory of counterfactuals. *Philosophy of Science*, 69(1):82–104.

Lange, M. (1999). Laws, counterfactuals, stability, and degrees of lawhood. *Philosophy of Science*, 66(2):243–267.

Lange, M. (2005). Laws and their stability. *Synthese*, 144(3):415–432.

Lange, M. (2009). *Laws and Lawmakers: Science, Metaphysics, and the Laws of Nature*. Oxford University Press.

Lange, M. (2013). Grounding, scientific explanation, and Humean laws. *Philosophical Studies*, 164(1):255–261.

Lange, M. (2016). *Because without Cause: Non-casual Explanations in Science and Mathematics*. Oxford University Press.

Lazarovici, D. (2018). Against fields. *European Journal for Philosophy of Science*, 8(2):145–170.

Lazarovici, D. (2020). Typical Humean worlds have no laws. *Manuscript. philsci-archive.pitt.edu/17469/*.

Lewis, D. (1973). *Counterfactuals*. Blackwell.

Lewis, D. (1979). Counterfactual dependence and time's arrow. *Noûs*, 13:455–476.

Lewis, D. (1980). A subjectivist's guide to objective chance. In Jeffrey, R. C., editor, *Studies in Inductive Logic and Probability*, volume 2, pages 263–293. University of California Press.

Lewis, D. (1983). New work for a theory of universals. *Australasian Journal of Philosophy*, 61:343–377.

Lewis, D. (1986). *Philosophical Papers II*. Oxford: Oxford University Press.

Lewis, D. (1994). Humean supervenience debugged. *Mind*, 103:473–490.

Loewer, B. (2001). Determinism and chance. *Studies in History and Philosophy of Science Part B: Studies in History and Philosophy of Modern Physics*, 32(4):609–620.

Loewer, B. (2007a). Counterfactuals and the second law. In Price, H. and Corry, R., editors, *Causation, Physics, and the Constitution of Reality: Russell's Republic Revisited*, pages 293–326. Oxford University Press.

Loewer, B. (2007b). Laws and natural properties. *Philosophical Topics*, 35(1/2):313–328.

Loewer, B. (2012). Two accounts of laws and time. *Philosophical Studies*, 160(1):115–137.

Loewer, B. (2020a). The consequence argument meets the Mentaculus. In Loewer, B., Winsberg, E., Brad Weslake, editor, *Time's Arrows and the Probability Structure of the world*. Harvard University Press, forthcoming.

Loewer, B. (2020b). The Mentaculus vision. In Allori, V., editor, *Statistical Mechanics and Scientific Explanation: Determinism, Indeterminism and Laws of Nature*, pages 3–29. World Scientific.

Loewer, B. (2020c). The package deal account of laws and properties (pda). *Synthese*, 199(1–2):1065–1089.

Loewer, B. (2021). What breathes fire into the equations. *Manuscript*.

Manchak, J. (2020). *Global Spacetime Structure*. Cambridge University Press.

Manchak, J. B. (2009). Can we know the global structure of spacetime? *Studies in History and Philosophy of Science Part B: Studies in History and Philosophy of Modern Physics*, 40(1):53–56.

Maudlin, T. (2007). *The Metaphysics within Physics*. Oxford University Press.

Maudlin, T. (2019). *Philosophy of Physics: Quantum Theory*, volume 9. Princeton University Press.

McKenzie, K. (2022). *Fundamentality and Grounding*. Cambridge University Press.

Meacham, C. J. (2023). The nomic likelihood account of laws. *Ergo*, 9, 230–284.

Miller, E. (2014). Quantum entanglement, Bohmian mechanics, and Humean supervenience. *Australasian Journal of Philosophy*, 92(3):567–583.

Montague, R. (1974). *Formal Philosophy: Selected Papers of Richard Montague*. Yale University Press.

Mumford, S. (2004). *Laws in Nature*. Routledge.

Myrvold, W. (2017). Philosophical issues in quantum theory. In Zalta, E. N., editor, *The Stanford Encyclopedia of Philosophy*. Metaphysics Research Lab, Stanford University, Spring 2017 edition.

North, J. (2021). *Physics, Structure, and Reality*. Oxford University Press.

Norton, J. D. (2019). The Hole Argument. In Zalta, E. N., editor, *The Stanford Encyclopedia of Philosophy*. Metaphysics Research Lab, Stanford University, Summer 2019 edition.

Page, D. N. (2009). Symmetric-bounce quantum state of the universe. *Journal of Cosmology and Astroparticle Physics*, 2009(9):026.

Penrose, R. (1974). The role of aesthetics in pure and applied mathematical research. *Bulletin of the Institute of Mathematics and Its Applications*, 10:266–271.

Penrose, R. (1979). Singularities and time-asymmetry. In Hawking, S. and Israel, W., editors, *General Relativity*, pages 581–638. Cambridge University Press.

Penrose, R. (1989). *The Emperor's New Mind: Concerning Computers, Minds, and the Laws of Physics*. Oxford University Press.

Roberts, J. T. (2008). *The Law-Governed Universe*. Oxford University Press.

Rovelli, C. (2019). Where was past low-entropy? *Entropy*, 21(5):466.

Russell, B. (1913). On the notion of cause. *Proceedings of the Aristotelian Society*, 13:1–26.

Sainsbury, R. M. (1990). Concepts without boundaries. *Inaugural Lecture Given at King's College London on 6 November 1990*.

Schaffer, J. (2016). It is the business of laws to govern. *dialectica*, 70(4):577–588.

Sorensen, R. (2018). Vagueness. In Zalta, E. N., editor, *The Stanford Encyclopedia of Philosophy*. Metaphysics Research Lab, Stanford University, Summer 2018 edition.

Sutherland, R. I. (2008). Causally symmetric Bohm model. *Studies in History and Philosophy of Science Part B: Studies in History and Philosophy of Modern Physics*, 39(4):782–805.

Tooley, M. (1977). The nature of laws. *Canadian Journal of Philosophy*, 7(4):667–698.

Uzan, J.-P. (2011). Varying constants, gravitation and cosmology. *Living Reviews in Relativity*, 14(1):1–155.

Vetter, B. (2015). *Potentiality: From Dispositions to Modality*. Oxford University Press.

Wallace, D. (2010). Gravity, entropy, and cosmology: In search of clarity. *The British Journal for the Philosophy of Science*, 513–540.

Weatherall, J. O. (2019a). Part 1: Theoretical equivalence in physics. *Philosophy Compass*, 14(5):e12592.

Weatherall, J. O. (2019b). Part 2: Theoretical equivalence in physics. *Philosophy Compass*, 14(5):e12591.

Weinberg, S. (1992). *Dreams of a Final Theory: The Search for the Fundamental Laws of Nature*. Pantheon.

Wheeler, J. A. and Feynman, R. P. (1945). Interaction with the absorber as the mechanism of radiation. *Reviews of Modern Physics*, 17(2–3):157.

Wheeler, J. A. and Feynman, R. P. (1949). Classical electrodynamics in terms of direct interparticle action. *Reviews of Modern Physics*, 21(3):425.

Wigner, E. (1985). Events, laws of nature, and invariance principles. In Zichichi, A., editor, *How Far Are We from the Gauge Forces – Proceedings of the 21st Course of the International School of Subnuclear Physics, Aug 3–14, 1983*, pages 699–708. Plenum.

Wigner, E. P. (1964). Symmetry and conservation laws. *Proceedings of the National Academy of Sciences of the United States of America*, 51(5):956–965.

Williams, P. (2023). *Philosophy of Particle Physics*. Cambridge University Press.

Woodward, J. and Ross, L. (2021). Scientific Explanation. In Zalta, E. N., editor, *The Stanford Encyclopedia of Philosophy*. Metaphysics Research Lab, Stanford University, Summer 2021 edition.

Acknowledgments

I am grateful to Sheldon Goldstein for invaluable discussions about laws of physics over many years. The topics in this Element are directly related to those explored in our joint paper on minimal primitivism (MinP). I thank Shelly Yiran Shi and Bosco Garcia for their research assistance and helpful comments on several earlier drafts, Tyler Hildebrand for stimulating discussions and valuable feedback, two anonymous reviewers of Cambridge University Press and the editor James Owen Weatherall for insightful comments. I am also grateful to Emily Adlam, David Albert, Jeffrey Barrett, Craig Callender, Eugene Chua, Christopher Dorst, Nina Emery, Ned Hall, James Hartle, Boris Kment, Marc Lange, Barry Loewer, Tim Maudlin, Chris Meacham, Kerry McKenzie, John Roberts, Carlo Rovelli, Charles Sebens, Elliott Sober, Eric Watkins, participants in the lecture series "Laws of Nature" at Wuhan University in September 2023 and the graduate seminar "Laws and Randomness" at UC San Diego in fall 2023. This project is supported by an Academic Senate Grant from UC San Diego.

Cambridge Elements ≡

The Philosophy of Physics

James Owen Weatherall
University of California, Irvine

James Owen Weatherall is Professor of Logic and Philosophy of Science at the University of California, Irvine. He is the author, with Cailin O'Connor, of *The Misinformation Age: How False Beliefs Spread* (Yale, 2019), which was selected as a *New York Times* Editors' Choice and Recommended Reading by *Scientific American*. His previous books were *Void: The Strange Physics of Nothing* (Yale, 2016) and the *New York Times* bestseller *The Physics of Wall Street: A Brief History of Predicting the Unpredictable* (Houghton Mifflin Harcourt, 2013). He has published approximately fifty peer-reviewed research articles in journals in leading physics and philosophy of science journals and has delivered over 100 invited academic talks and public lectures.

About the Series

This Cambridge Elements series provides concise and structured introductions to all the central topics in the philosophy of physics. The Elements in the series are written by distinguished senior scholars and bright junior scholars with relevant expertise, producing balanced, comprehensive coverage of multiple perspectives in the philosophy of physics.

Cambridge Elements ☰

The Philosophy of Physics